FOCUS YOUR LOCUS

ACTIVITIES THAT FOCUS THE POWER OF INDIVIDUALS AND GROUPS

Mike Gessford • Justin McGlamery

Published by:

Wood 'N' Barnes Publishing
2309 N. Willow, Bethany, OK 73008
(405) 942-6812
woodnbarnes.com

Cover Art by Blue Designs
Copyediting & Layout Design by Ramona Cunningham
Photographs by Rebecca Earl
Additional Photography by Jarrad McGlamery (p. 68)
Mike Gessford (p. 40 & 78)

Printed in the United States of America
Bethany, Oklahoma
ISBN # 978-1-885473-89-9

For Chip—
the ultimate locus focuser.
Now that's a TORB!

Acknowledgements

There are many people without whom this book could not be possible. Many years of learning our craft, inspired by many skilled facilitators, shared with many people, have made this a labor of love and a very memorable experience.

We have to thank our friend Rich Keegan, who has encouraged us from the beginning, traveled the entire path with us from the inception of this book, serving as our official roadie at conferences, our unofficial agent and partner in many instances of "failing forward."

Chris Ortiz also deserves big thanks for being with us from the beginning of the concept for this book. We are both in awe of his game-smithing ability, but mostly appreciate Chris for his humor, playfulness, and eye for fun.

We need to thank Bernie Lindauer, the director of the Gengras Center, for his patience and understanding and for empowering us with the time and schedule to be able to follow our passion for adventure education. We'd also like to thank all the Gengras Center staff and students through the years for playing along with us and trusting our faith in unknown outcomes. You have taught us many lessons that have shaped our practice.

We owe special gratitude and thanks to Betsy Collins, an original member of the adventure education staff at the Gengras Center who has always been there for us. Her positive and thoughtful ways set a wonderful tone during many an adventure education group. Also thanks to Arlette Cassidy, who is our adventure-trained school psychologist. By enlightening our world with the magic of mirror neurons, she has given us a scientific basis on which to focus as we explore with our groups and has guided some of the research that made this book take the form that it has.

We would like to thank Billye Auclair, Academic Dean at Saint Joseph College, who understands the positive outcomes that experiential education can bring to a college community. Billye made it possible for us to pursue our vision of moving this style of teaching into the college's academic world.

We must also thank Cheryl Barnard, Dean of Students, and the Student Affairs staff who have enthusiastically welcomed us into their space and made us feel at home as we build this particular part of the Saint Joseph College signature experience.

We must give praise to the entire Renbrook Summer Adventure ropes staff. Working on the ropes course each summer with such professionals has been part of our adult continuing education. We have been blessed with lifelong friends with whom we've learned, taught, inspired, and laughed way too much to be getting paid.

We owe a special thanks to Doug Cramphin. Long since working with Doug at Renbrook, he has continued to honor us by letting us infiltrate his life and teaching with adventure education experiences. We are grateful for his ability to be a lifelong learner and can only hope to match his energy as we continue to learn and facilitate.

Thanks to the great folks who showed up for the Hocus Pocus Focus Your Locus workshop pictured in this book. Your beautiful spirits and faces make this book come alive and we love that you were there. Of course, you can have all the photogenic people in all the right places, but if there is no skilled photographer to capture the image, the moment is lost. We owe a huge thanks to Rebecca Earl for her patience, enthusiasm, flexibility, and ability to get just the right shots to illustrate the activities in this book. Her selfless work took a lot of stress off our plates and allowed us to just be ourselves.

We'd like to thank everyone who selflessly gave his or her time and effort to review this book. Your feedback and suggestions have proven to be both helpful and insightful.

None of this would have been possible without the expertise and hard work of our publishing company, Wood 'N' Barnes, and our editor, Mony Cunningham. Mony took two first-time authors, instilled us with confidence, and then trusted us to be ourselves. We also thank David Wood and Micah Jacobson for their insightful feedback to our initial submission and giving us a direction that helped us become more concise. It has been a wonderful lesson in collaboration and trust as we see the book in its final format.

We owe a big thanks and debt of gratitude to Jen Stanchfield. We always seemed to be presenting at conferences in the same time slots. When she finally was able to attend a session of ours, she suggested that this workshop actually had the makings of a book. We were happily surprised at her suggestion, having never really considered taking these ideas this far. Jen facilitated our journey through the process and encouraged us the whole way. Of course, that's just Jen being Jen.

Mike's personal acknowledgements:

I'd like to take an opportunity to thank Tom Quimby. Tom was my adventure education teacher in both high school and college. My whole foundation in this field comes from TQ. I can truly say that he was my inspiration for getting into this field and for continuing to learn and grow as an educator.

I would like to recognize both of my grandfathers, authors themselves, for instilling a love of words and language in me. I would like to thank my parents, Dave and Sandy Gessford, both educators, in different ways, for all their love and support. Much love goes to my daughter and son, Molly and David, for their sense of fun and also for accepting their dad as someone who occasionally looks at life through a playful lens. I also need to send the biggest thanks to my wife Judy. She admits that while she doesn't fully understand what I do for a living, she knows that it is important to me to let the lines between my personal and professional life be blurred by fun. Thanks Judy, for your love and for letting me play.

Justin's personal acknowledgements:

Thank you to Don Jones for your probing, interesting questions along the way, which truly helped my process greatly.

Thank you Mom, I love you, and again... I owe you big time!

Thanks to my entire family; Dad, WJ, Saide, I love you.

Much love and thanks to the Lubensteins and Ettelmans, too. I love being a part your crazy family.

I would also like to thank the Gruber family. You took me in as your own and saw the potential in me, and I consider all of you my family, too.

Thank you to my brothers from another mother; Pauley, Jeff, and Damion, you cats are my soul brothers. We have learned, and continue to learn so much together. Also, much love and shout outs to the Dilots. We were professional players, and you all helped shape my sense of play and who I am.

Last, but most certainly not least, thank you to my most inner circle, my family; Rayne, Naiyah, and Taj, you guys are my whole world. I am so proud of all of you and love watching you become who you are. The biggest and deepest thank you to Jarrad, my wife, my love, my partner, my friend; your support and patience through this process has been unbelievable. You are the best. Soul Love.

Content

Introduction

Have you ever led a group or had a class where things seemed to be going along just fine and then suddenly they were stuck and floundering? Have you ever had a group that was "so close, yet so far away"? Have you wondered why? What do you do with them? Can you create that breakthrough moment that assists them to get back on track?

Often, when working in teams, once focus is lost, performance deteriorates. Poor performance often leads to low morale, which can, in turn, lead to poor attitudes and to personality-driven conflicts, throwing the group back into the storming and dysfunctional stages of group development. What can we do as teachers, as group leaders and facilitators to help refocus our groups and harness the necessary energy to keep the momentum moving through the experiential learning cycle? Understanding the energy within us is important. Being able to harness and focus the collective power of the group can bring groups back to previous levels of performance and then move them far beyond.

Focus enables people to more clearly access their thoughts. Access to one's thoughts helps individuals to evaluate previous thoughts and experiences and create new ideas. New ideas create energy. Energy stimulates awareness, which can influence where one's locus of control resides. Awareness can fuel courage, potentially allowing one to become more individually responsible. Courage leads to an enhanced ability to make new conscious choices, which, when made within groups, lead to mutual accountability. These new choices lead to new opportunities for learning and growth. New learning and experiences provide opportunities for new thoughts, and the cycle begins anew, with focus enabling people to access their thoughts more clearly.*

---

* See page 137 for a graphic of this learning cycle.

One of the greatest resources in our lives is the power of our minds. That is why, if we want to get the most use out of this power, understanding the brain's functioning and abilities is an important place to begin. Later in this book, we will discuss some recent brain-based research about mirror neurons and the roles they may play in group focus and collective experiences. We will also look at how the positive effects of play support the usefulness of the activities presented to increase focus, team performance, and the ability to have that "aha" moment.

It is our goal to provide opportunities for you to learn, relearn, or rethink some active and reflective activities that can be relevant for all types of counselors, teachers, and experiential educators. The activities illustrate the power of the focused individual and of the collective mind. We will explore how our brain is working when we use experiential activities to bring the group back to a state of elevated concentration. Some of the methods discussed can be used to front-load learning, to sustain group momentum, to energize initiatives, and to provide new streams of insight during processing.

While this book will provide many suggestions and activities both old and new, it is not intended as a quick fix, but rather as a collection of ideas that have worked well with our groups. Every group is different, made of unique individuals with unique talents and issues, which require many skillsets for different circumstances. We invite you to journey with us as we explore "focus," and some new slants on how to think about group facilitation.

Mike & Justin

The Genesis of
Hocus Pocus, Focus Your Locus

Adventure education is something that we are passionate about. It is a philosophy and methodology in which educators purposefully engage with learners in direct experience and focused reflection in order to increase knowledge, develop skills, and clarify values. We were lucky to discover this passion early in life and even more fortunate to be able to have a place to work that allows us to pursue these passions. This process of learning and methodology of facilitating learning is something we have come to believe in. That is why we wanted to write this book. These activities work. This style of teaching and learning is significant. We've seen evidence of its significance over and over. It's as simple as that. This isn't rocket science, and we're not solving the global climate crisis, but the outcomes and realizations that people have continually found through active, hands-on learning appear to be very important to many diverse groups of people. It is the passion for this style of learning that fuels the many different visions of a wide variety of groups and individuals.

One way this has been demonstrated to us is by looking at the distinctly different routes that brought the two of us to work together and write this book. We both grew up as curious kids, aware of and immersed in the popular cultures of our respective times. The paths we took were somewhat different. As adolescents, I, Mike, was more of a rule follower and Justin was more of a rule challenger. The roads we chose were divergent in that way. Some might say mine was more traditional and Justin's nontraditional. Yet, we each had experiences, shared with others, that led us to that "aha" moment of realizing that helping others to reach their potential was what we wanted to do with our lives. We both cared deeply about the relationships we developed with the people around us. This was our common ground.

How We Came Together

Allow me to give you a little background information: I first met Justin as a teenager while his father and I were working together. We became colleagues when we started working at the Gengras Center. I had been working there about 10 years when Justin joined our staff. I find it fascinating in retrospect that we ended up working closely together. I am very grateful for Justin's many gifts. Our yin and yang complement each other well, and we value our close relationship.

In 1987, I became the first full-time physical education teacher at the Gengras Center. The Gengras Center is a school for about 125 special needs students, ages 5 to 21. It is located on the campus of Saint Joseph College in West Hartford, Connecticut. Through the years, I observed that the profile of our student population was changing. As the students arrived with fewer language and physical skills, I sensed that there had to be a better way to teach them the necessary skills to participate successfully in their personal recreational activities.

The obvious solution to me was to return to my roots in adventure education, which was based in cooperation, not competition. This style of hands-on learning, for individuals as well as groups, in an outdoor setting produced some remarkable results. We didn't always know why it happened, but we knew we had a tiger by the tail with this form of teaching and learning. It was clear and simple to me. I had again found the rush of being a teacher who made a difference. Justin had similar feelings with his experience.

What made it even better this time was that the students realized the lessons were the kinds of things that transcended sports and other recreational activities. The insights were concepts that they could take back to all other areas of their lives and apply each day. It was also experiencing those "aha" moments as a group, going beyond the individual experience. It wasn't the skill itself, but how each person used his/her skill to make the team or group better and stronger. It was the building of trust and the resulting relationships that mattered so much. I am very happy with the direction this piece of curriculum took. It pays to listen to your heart.

Workshop

Regional and international conferences have become an important part of my lifelong learning. They are where I learn new activities, discuss industry-wide standards, and receive many reaffirmations of things I have learned previously. The most important part of these conferences has become the people I encounter and get to know. I hear the stories and wisdom of people who have been in this profession even before it had a name. It is this networking that reinvigorates me and leads to unexpected treasures and opportunities.

The workshop that inspired this book was born out of a couple of informal discussions Justin and I had with Rich Keegan and Chris Ortiz over dinner at the Association of Experiential Education (AEE) International Conference in Minneapolis, Minnesota in November of 2006. We talked about some common summer camp experiences. During our conversations, Justin and I explained that in our programs, we "levitate" people to show the power that a group has within it. This is not the type of levitation that often follows "Willow in the Wind," where a whole group raises a prone person up to chest height and then lowers him back down to the ground. Rather, this type of levitation has a seated person lifted up by four other group members, using only two fingers each.

We returned to the hotel where some of the evening's entertainment was going on, and met up with some other folks and shared our conversations with them. There was some skepticism and they wanted to "see it to believe it." We adjourned to a large common area outside of where the band was playing and started to facilitate the activity. With Justin's flair for the dramatic, he took the facilitation lead. Rich, Chris, and I jumped into the supporting roles of lifters and spotters. As people were raised out of the chair, they had looks of shock and amazement on their faces. We decided right then that this might be something to build a workshop around.

Another chance meeting at that conference led to the discovery and development of an activity that has become a mainstay of our Hocus Pocus workshops. We met up with a young woman named Becky Disciacca and her colleague, Kate, before one of the keynote addresses. As we were waiting for the talk to begin we noticed that they each had a piece of string, about a foot long, with a washer tied to the end. These little pendulums have evolved into one of the centerpieces of our workshop for focusing individuals.

Once we realized that we had a collection of activities for a workshop, we started thinking about a name. We had always been attracted to the workshops with clever-sounding names or tag lines. We aspired to something like that. "Focus" was the buzzword that kept coming up. The "hocus pocus" part seemed to come fairly easily, but it took awhile before the word "locus" popped into my head. It took about two seconds for us to put these words together in their current order. We thought the name sounded even Seussical, was pretty interesting, and would catch the attention of others. We looked up the definition from a couple of different sources to see if the word "locus" indeed was what we wanted.

The American Heritage Dictionary defines locus as "A center or focus of great activity or intense concentration." Dictionary.com* defines locus as "A center or source, as of activities or power: locus of control." I like both of these definitions. The American Heritage version seems to suggest that the focus from the locus of control is an outward one (external locus of control), while Dictionary.com seems to indicate the focus from the locus of control is more from within (internal locus of control). This is useful, as we used both of those types of focus during our activities; the outward focus that deals more with how an individual is functioning in a group, and the inner focus that deals more with how an individual is concentrating on his/her own behavior. Thus, our workshop, "Hocus Pocus, Focus Your Locus" was born.

Book

The idea of writing a book that incorporated ideas from our workshop was first proposed to us by Jen Stanchfield. After our initial reactions of surprise and excitement, the concept started to take shape. Our goal was to put together a collection of activities and thoughts that could become another resource for facilitators to use in making meaningful connections for their participants. We feel that this is the true essence of experiential education.

This book addresses concepts and activities for the individual as well as the group. The relationship between the two is equally important, dependent, and vital for our groups to grow and our communities to thrive. While facilitating, Justin and I keep coming back to the terms "individual responsibility" and "mutual accountability." People who understand the nature of the relationship between the two usually encounter more success within the groups they belong to. Because of the nature of experiential education, learning from your mistakes, or "failing forward," is encouraged and supported. As educational leaders, facilitators, or instructors, the fine line we always seem to be walking is how much leeway to

---

* Locus definition/dictionary.com. Retrieved November 11, 2006, from dictionary. com Web site: http://dictionary.reference.com/browse/Locus

give individuals or groups in finding their own way and reflecting upon their experiences. It is a delicate balancing act. We have found from experience that, when you or your group seems to be floundering a little bit, you are often the last to know. Sometimes, an activity introduced from outside the sphere of your group's concentration is just the trigger you need to see things with more clarity than before, thus the "aha" moment. Of course, it isn't as simple as I make it seem right here. Conversely, allowing a group to work a problem through is desirable, as long as the members keep their conflict issue driven and not personality driven. Hence, the fine dividing line between the task and the art of facilitation.

At the 2006 AEE International Conference in Minneapolis, Minnesota, I attended a workshop that was also attended by Craig Dobkin, an inspirational, highly experienced educator. Something he said that day paints an accurate picture of why we do what we do: "A picture is worth a thousand words, but experience is worth a thousand pictures." We hope that you will try some of these activities, and through that experience, gain a sense of the power and possible outcomes that might occur. As you gain comfort in facilitating them, you should acquire a sense of purpose for each of them, knowing what outcomes they are likely to bring. Having a purpose for each of your activities gives you commitment and confidence.

In regard to this book, we must make the claim that we are not social scientists or researchers. Although we understand the need for scientifically based studies to validate the practices of our facilitation, this is not the primary goal of what we are trying to accomplish here. Indeed, that would be beyond our skills and unfair to others to make such claims. It is our goal to merely relay our experiences as a backdrop for you to compare and contrast with your own. We always say to the classes and groups we work with that, "We are not experts. We stand to learn just as much from you as you might from us." That remains true to this day.

Because we all have a locus of control, in one form or another, in the next chapter we will examine the common energy that flows through all of us. This will give us common ground as we further explore individual and group energy.

Come on, Energy! (Common Energy)

2

Since the dawn of recorded history, shamans and healers from every corner of the world have alluded to the energy that we as humans both create and emit. There are many words used to describe the energy that flows through each of us. Some call it chi, some call it prana, some life force, and some call it just plain old verve. Quantum physics describes the universe as energy and states that energy and matter are interchangeable. String theory suggests that differences in matter are just variations in energy vibrations. However you choose to look at energy, whether it be through a scientific or spiritual lens, all perspectives respected, it is undeniable that we, as humans and living beings on the Earth, at the very least, create and conduct energy.

Some people claim to actually be able to see this energy, often referred to as an aura. However, for most people, this layer of subtle energy, as it is referred to in some academic circles, remains unseen by the naked eye. It was Semyon Kirlian, a Russian researcher, who discovered an interesting photographic technique in 1940, now called Kirlian photography, that actually captured the electromagnetic energy field that surrounds living things in the form of a photograph. For those of us who need to see something to believe it, this is it. We can actually see the energy field that surrounds and permeates living things. Kirlian's technique was to place a photographic plate between an object, such as a leaf, and a specially designed electrode emitting a specific frequency (Hz). The movement of the billions of charged electrons emitting from the object was captured on the film. When the film was processed, brilliantly colored coronas, much like those of the sun during an eclipse, were captured creating an electromagnetic image similar to the photographed object. What was most surprising, in the case of the leaf, was that although a partial or torn leaf was photo-

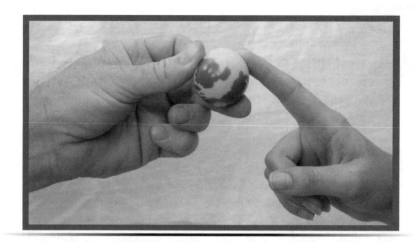

graphed, the Kirlian image showed the electromagnetic image of the whole leaf. Although the leaf had lost part of its physical self, the energy that it emitted still showed it as whole. Similar experiments have been done with humans, photographing the meridian points used in acupuncture, showing the blocking and flowing of energy between and through these points. We can now actually see this energy.

As much as I wish that we had one of these incredibly cool sounding devices to demonstrate the human energy field, we do not. We are far more low tech! For our groups, we use a simple circuit in the form of a ping-pong ball with electrodes and an LED light for an activity we call Energy Ball, which is described in detail on pages 19 and 20.

I have long thought that we are all part of something bigger than ourselves. Now, before you close the book saying, "Oh boy, here we go with some way-out kook stuff!" just consider the thoughts conveyed here. It is not our intent to change anyone's mind or challenge anyone's faith, merely to ponder some possibilities. The beautiful part about the possibilities we will explore is that they may support what you already know or believe to be true. They may contradict your belief system and if that is the case, please know that you can still have a positive effect from using these activities and information, just as one may have from taking a placebo medication.

I preface this in this way because we have had very strong reactions from some of the activities we use. Because these activities demonstrate the collective power of a focused group and illustrate that in a very powerful, visual, and at times visceral way, we have actually been accused of using voodoo. I assure you this is not the case. There is nothing dark about what we do, and all faiths are welcome and encouraged to try these activities and put the information discussed in this book to the test. We would love to hear about how the activities work or don't work for you, as well as any variations or twists you may find useful for specific groups with specific belief systems.

I truly believe that as children, we are very tuned in to the collective consciousness, to the energy of the universe, whatever you want to call it, and that as we get older and are taught fear and begin to conform and pay attention to TV and things less natural, we are socialized into thinking that these connections are imaginings, fantastical, dreamed up, the stuff that kooks believe, and the like. I think we are all far more connected than we either realize or would like to believe.

Perhaps it is easier to rationalize so much of the selfishness that we as humans engage in regularly if we deny these connections. If we are connected, than the wrongs and injustices that either we commit, or that the companies we work for commit, or the governments of the countries in which we live commit, affect us as well. It is easier to look at the immediate gratification we receive in the short run—profit, power, status, and so forth—than it is to realize that what goes around comes around and that all we do affects everything. That is a huge responsibility!

Almost every religion has spoken to the notion of the Ethic of Reciprocity in each of its respective holy books, whether it be called the golden rule (Christianity), "the sum of the Dharma (duty)" (Hinduism), Doctrine of the Mean 13.3 (Confucianism), Number 13 of Imam Al-Nawawi's *Forty Hadith* (Islam), the list actually could go on an on. The point being, we, as people, and let's even take it a step beyond, we as living things in the universe, are sharing this moment in time right now, and simply because of that, we are experiencing a commonality. We all have the same basic needs and all share common desires: to be healthy and loved. Now, if that is not a strong enough connection and commonality, then I don't know what is.

Gandhi said, "Be the change you wish to see in the world."

I think this puts it quite nicely. This says that we each have the responsibility to change things; that the locus of control resides within each of us and within our belief systems. If we are the change we wish to see, then we are being individually responsible, both to and for ourselves and our respective beliefs, which enables us to be mutually accountable to the world and to all those whom we believe need to change as well.

Of the many great books I read as a teenager, one that has influenced my thinking on the subject of collective consciousness is *The Hundredth Monkey* by Ken Keyes, Jr. The following is an excerpt from his book.

> *The Japanese monkey,* Macaca fuscata, *has been observed in the wild for a period of over 30 years. In 1952, on the island of Koshima scientists were providing monkeys with sweet potatoes dropped in the sand. The monkeys liked the taste of the raw sweet potatoes, but they found the dirt unpleasant.*
>
> *An 18-month-old female named Imo found she could solve the problem in a nearby stream. She taught this trick to her mother. Her playmates also learned this new way and they taught their mothers, too. This cultural innovation was gradually picked up by various monkeys before the eyes of the scientists.*
>
> *Between 1952 and 1958, all the young monkeys learned to wash the sandy sweet potatoes to make them more palatable. Only the adults who imitated their children learned this social improvement. Other adults kept eating the dirty sweet potatoes.*
>
> *Then something startling took place. In the autumn of 1958, a certain number of Koshima monkeys were washing sweet potatoes—the exact number is not known. Let us suppose that when*

the sun rose one morning there were 99 monkeys on Koshima Island who had learned to wash their sweet potatoes. Let's further suppose that later that morning, the hundredth monkey learned to wash potatoes.

THEN IT HAPPENED!

By that evening almost everyone in the tribe was washing sweet potatoes before eating them. The added energy of this hundredth monkey somehow created an ideological breakthrough!

But notice. A most surprising thing observed by these scientists was that the habit of washing sweet potatoes then jumped over the sea... Colonies of monkeys on other islands and the mainland troop of monkeys at Takasakiyama began washing their sweet potatoes!

Thus, when a certain critical number achieves an awareness, this new awareness may be communicated from mind to mind. Although the exact number may vary, the Hundredth Monkey Phenomenon means that when only a limited number of people know of a new way, it may remain the conscious property of these people. But there is a point at which if only one more person tunes in to a new awareness, a field is strengthened so that this awareness is picked up by almost everyone!...

You may be the "Hundredth Monkey"...

The Hundredth Monkey had a very profound effect on my thinking then, and still does to this day. I immediately thought, "Wow! There has to be something to this!" I tucked this story away in the back of my brain, embraced it as something I believed to be true, and began to live my life with this concept in mind.

Years passed, and in 2001, I went to my first formal adventure-based counseling training at Project Adventure in Beverly, Massachusetts. The five-day workshop was awesome! The trainers were both great, and I felt as if I had come home. The large group of participants was split into two smaller groups of about ten, and my smaller group was comprised of about eight American men and women, one Chinese woman who spoke very little English, and an Italian man who spoke even less English. Our group became hyper-aware of how to communicate in this situation. The language barrier caused all of the English speakers to rethink just about everything they said in order to communicate to the non-English speakers in a way they could understand. This caused us to really understand what it was we were all trying to say even more. We became able to communicate without talking, understanding just about every-thing anyone was trying to say, simply through intention. Now there were some non-verbals that we all established meanings for, but we began to relate on a higher level than just words. We became a very high-performing group very quickly and just when I was making the connection to the rest of my life and belief system, our facilitator, Carol James, read us *The Hundredth Monkey*. I was reawakened. This became a defining moment in my life. This was one of those times when what you believe to be true is played back to you in another form and reaffirms that what you know to be true actually is. I knew at that moment that this was the field I needed to work in and that I was walking on the right path. When the uni-verse opens up a door for you and you see that opening, walk on through. I was the hundredth monkey again on that day.

Now, while some skeptics have taken to demystifying the hun-dredth monkey effect, I believe I have seen this phenomenon and began observing it in action, both positively as well as negatively. Let's examine this on a purely theoretical level for a moment. I believe that this phenomenon has everything to do with the collec-tive consciousness on a metaphysical level, and mirror neurons on a neuroscientific physical level. Take the monkey Imo for example. Imo learned, perhaps serendipitously, that the sweet potatoes would taste better without the sand in her teeth. She then began intentionally washing them and eating them. Did she intention-ally "teach" her mother and her contemporaries to do the same, or did they learn by "mirroring" the same actions? At the time *The Hundredth Monkey* was written, behavioral science and psychology didn't know about the existence of mirror neurons. However, re-cent research may suggest that this learned or taught behavior was done through imitation: monkey see, monkey do. More on this thought later. Therein lies the explanation of the learning done on the immediate level of Imo's group and location. Now, once the new knowledge jumped to another island, we get to the discussion about intention and collective consciousness.

To relate this all back to energy and common energy, we need to discuss for a moment the concept that everything is energy. If everything is indeed energy, then thoughts and ideas are, too. As Keyes suggests with the hundredth monkey phenomenon, once a certain number of beings hold the same consciousness, awareness (energy), it can shift and its energy field strengthens and can be acquired more easily by others because it has been given the power of intentionality, the power of belief. This concept has been beautifully and remarkably illustrated through the work of a Japanese researcher and author named Masaru Emoto.

Have you ever thought about the power of words? I mean, we all have heard the old saying, "The pen is mightier than the sword." Well, many believe there may actually be scientific proof to back that up now. One of the things we discuss in groups all the time is the importance of communication. Communication, as we all know, can take on many forms, but let us discuss just the written or spoken word for a moment. Words obviously have meanings. Meanings are essentially intentions, and speaking to intention, we can say the same word with different intention, or merely a different inflection, and affect the word's meaning, changing the effect of the initial intention of the word. What Emoto has discovered has reaffirmed what I already believe to be true but has also completely changed my way of looking at words, at intention. Emoto began researching water. He initially took samples of water that originated from the same source: at the source of the spring, where the water came out of the earth; midstream, after the water had flowed as streams and rivers through wilderness and civilization; and at its last state, as fresh water, just before it emptied into the Sea of Osaka. Emoto collected these samples, stored them in identical containers, and took them back to his lab. Emoto and his researchers then took drops of each sample and placed them on slides to view and photograph under a microscope. The lab was kept at a constant minus-five degrees Celsius, as the goal was to capture the image of the water drop once it had frozen. What

Emoto found was astounding. The water drops from the sample taken at the source of the stream formed into beautifully symmetrical hexagonally shaped ice crystals, each different, much like snowflakes. The water that had been taken from midstream, and at the point where it emptied into the sea was hardly able to form into a complete crystal. After passing through forests and the decaying plant and animal matter, the cities and towns, and all of the pollutants that accompany civilization, the water had changed. As Emoto said in his book, *The Healing Power of Water* (2008), "This was visible proof that not all water was the same—it reacted to the 'experiences' it went through during its journey and stored that information."

Emoto and his researchers took the information of the environmental and pollutant effects on water to another level and began to experiment with music and the effect it may have on the structural arrangement of water molecules. He put samples of the same distilled water into containers of the exact same type and exposed each sample to a different type of music. Again, the results were astounding. The structural arrangement of the water changed, and changed differently from each type of music it was exposed to. Emoto then took this to an entirely different level. If environment, pollutants, and even music (sound) can change the molecular structure of the water, then what about words and thoughts? He then, again, taking samples from the same distilled water, placed the water into identical vials, but this time attached different words printed out by a computer to each of the vials and left them overnight. The same procedure was performed for each of the various vials; each was shaken and tapped the same amount of times before extracting the water to drop onto the slide. Again, most interesting and awe-striking results were found. The vials containing water that had words of positive intention, such as "love," or "thank you," or "lucky" produced drops that were able to form into beautiful and symmetrical ice crystals, while the vials with negative words, like "demon," or "you fool," or "I hate you" formed misshapen crystals or were not able to fully form a crystal at all.

Emoto used his methods to test the effects of intention, thoughts, and prayers on water as well, with results consistent with his other experiments, suggesting that even the unspoken word—intention alone—can and does change water.

Now, again, lets take this to another level. We all know that water is directly connected to all life on this planet. We all enter this world comprised of roughly 90% water. Eventually, as we mature and are exposed to air and no longer exist entirely in water, as we did in the womb, we become about 70% water, roughly the same amount that covers the body of the planet. If the written word can affect the structural arrangement of a drop of water on a slide in a lab, what happens to the water that comprises each of us? We all know how we are emotionally affected by the words that we either say or are said to us, especially when delivered with specific intention, so what about our molecular structure? Think about the potential implications of this for a moment. If words, simply printed out and taped to vials of water, affect change to the structural arrangement of that water's molecules, then what about the statements we wear on our clothing? What about the words we speak daily?

Think about how it feels to be told you are loved. I imagine it makes you feel similar to how it makes me feel: warm, safe, and accepted. Now think about how it makes you feel to speak those words, those same intentions. Similarly, I bet it makes you feel good! Conversely, when we speak in anger, or use words of hateful or fearful intent, we feel bad. I am always shocked at the level of aggressiveness people feel toward one another while sharing space on the highway. Granted, it is a life-or-death situation if something goes wrong. But when one experiences road rage, making a rude gesture and yelling obscenities at you, I imagine that while he may feel an immediate release of some sort, it is not making him feel any better. What does it do physically? It is actually poisoning him, affecting the structure of his very being and as a result, yours, because, as discussed earlier, we are all connected.

I mentioned earlier that words could simply be the written form of intentions. Do you see where I am going with this? If words are intention, then it is possible that even our intention or thoughts may affect us. Let's combine two of the discussed concepts now. If intention or thought can affect the structural arrangement of water molecules, and if we are mostly water, and if everything is energy, including thoughts and ideas, then it may also be possible that everything we think or say affects everything else on some level, both physically and energetically.

In my reading of Emoto, I was again brought back to a realization that this was information pertinent to my life. In the introduction of his book, *The Healing Power of Water*, Emoto too discusses the hundredth monkey phenomenon. Ah... clean sweet potatoes and clean intention! Nothing like clarity!

Now, I need to point out here, that Emoto has been criticized by the scientific community for his research methods and has had a million-dollar gauntlet thrown down to prove his research through peer-reviewed, double-blind studies. Let us assume for a moment that Emoto's work, which has sparked so much interest and excitement, is pseudoscience and not scientifically valid. Is it not enough that believing in something positive and well-intended can have a positive effect? The power of belief is nothing to scoff at. People the world over have had powerful physical and spiritual healing simply by placing their belief in something. Even if it is merely a placebo effect, the outcome is what we desire: health, love, gratitude, a better way of life, or what have you. Simply directing our thoughts, our energy, in a positive direction may change not only the way we think about things but also how we approach things and how we live our lives.

To tie all this back to facilitation, teaching, counseling, and to the groups with which we work, I think we need to be very mindful of the words and intention we bring to our groups. The energy we bring and the messages we wish to convey come across even without speaking. Are we creating barriers or opening doors for optimum learning? Our nonverbal communication and intention are picked up vibrationally even when people are not consciously aware of them. Just as we need to be mindful of our own energy, we need to be aware of taking on the energy of others. We will encounter many different people and subsequently, many different energies. As conscious people, we need to be sure that the energy we give off is that of the best intention, that it will have a positive effect on whomever we encounter. Once we are aware that this energy exists and that we directly impact one another, we also need to be aware that we have control over our own energy and that we can choose not to take on energy that is harmful to us. The more we become aware, the more we can master this.

We have all had those groups. You know, the ones that just seem to never get it. The day starts off and someone is dragging the rest of the group down. That person's attitude and energy affects everyone and by the end of the day, even though you've delivered a decent program, lesson plan, or session, and even though the group has had some fun and some good learning moments, everyone, including you, is completely drained. This is because of the exchanges of energy that have occurred throughout the day. Now of course there are many different levels to what could be affecting this outcome (some of these concepts and theories are discussed in the other chapters of this book), but take into consideration the impact energy has on us all. We are dealing with people in, at times, very contrived situations that seem to bring up all kinds of interpersonal dynamics. Even though the activities and problem-solving initiatives themselves have no real importance or relevance to our lives, the dynamics that present themselves do hold great importance. It is critical that we help group members understand the impact they are having on one another and how to connect these realizations to the rest of their lives. If they are acting a certain way during a silly, contrived activity, chances are this is how they behave, on some level, most of the time. Plato said, "You can learn more about a person in one hour of play than in a year of conversation." When we play, we are transported back to the child within, back to where our core values reside. Our true selves come out. Our job, as facilitators of learning, is to help people make connections to the other parts of their lives, giving these experiences meaning.

We can use these learning opportunities to help people reflect on their actions, words, and intentions and how they affect the rest of the group. Using proper sequencing and participant-directed processing methods, we can help them discover these realizations for themselves, allowing the group and individuals to have that "aha" moment—allowing somebody to be the hundredth monkey that day.

Before we turn to discussing other concepts, let's look at some activities that can bring up discussions about energy and how it affects the group process. These activities can act as energizers, as they are designed to get the group going, energized, and focused back on the same point.

As our groups arrive and we have that "perfect" plan in mind for their day, it is important to have a few activities in your back pocket to pull out in case you need to adjust your sequencing. We have found that starting off with icebreakers to get everyone loose and laughing, followed by some quick energizer activities really helps us gauge where the group is in its level of playfulness and energy. This helps us determine whether or not we stick to our original plan or shift a bit, allowing group members to take a different path. There have to be literally hundreds of energizer activities; however, we'd like to mention a few with which we have had great success.

Energy Ball

Contributor/History

This is a little gem we picked up from Karl Rohnke at the High 5 Adventure Learning Center's Annual Adventure Practitioners Symposium in 2004.

Concept/Objective

We use this activity to demonstrate that we are all connected, and that we all create and conduct energy within our groups.

Props/Materials Needed/Preparation

You need an Energy Ball, sometimes called a UFO Energy Ball. We also have a few World Energy Balls that look like the Earth. These can be purchased at various science stores or from folks in the field who sell props.

Directions/Scenarios/Instructions

Basically, the Energy Ball is a ping-pong ball with two small metal electrodes. When the electrodes are touched simultaneously, the circuit is closed and the ball lights up, flashes, and makes a "wooo-wooo" sound. It is a great toy for bringing to life a science lesson about open and closed circuits. It is also a great visual to illustrate that we are all connected and that energy flows through the group.

- Have the participants stand in a circle, close enough to eventually hold hands. Instruct them to hold their hands out in front of them, palms open and facing each other.

- Have them clap their hands and rub their palms together vigorously to generate and harness their energy. (I usually make a *Karate Kid* reference here, relating the motion to the scene when Mr. Miyagi performs the same action to heal Daniel-san's hurt knee.) Participants continue this motion until everyone has done it and the energy is beginning to become apparent.

- Now have group members join hands, making sure that everyone is connected only by hands and that no other connections are made. Hold the ball, making contact with one of the electrodes, and ask the person on either side of you to touch the other electrode. The ball should make noise and light up, and so should the group!

- We use this opportunity to talk about energy and being connected, about being present and being focused. Ask for someone to disconnect. With the loss of connection, the sound and lights stop—a great way to demonstrate how our actions within a group affect the entire group.

Ah! So! Zoo!
(or Ah, So, Ko!)
(or High, Low, Yo!)

Contributor/History

This oldie but goodie comes from Karl Rohnke's books, *FUNN Stuff # 1* and *FUNN 'n Games.*

Concept/Objective

This game is one that Rohnke says is just FUNN (Functional Understanding Not Necessary), however, I think this activity can be both a focuser as well as an energizer.

Props/Materials Needed/Preparation

No props needed.

Directions/Scenarios/Instructions

- The game starts with everyone in a circle. I usually tell the group that this is an ancient Eastern ritual used to focus power for the group and that it is most serious in nature (the seriousness won't last long!). Explain that an impulse will be passed around the group, and as it travels, it will pick up more and more positive energy.

- The game begins with learning the three sounds, "ah," "so," and "zoo," along with a corresponding motion for each sound. The first sound is "ah," and the corresponding motion is a salute with the whole hand flat, and the index finger brought quickly to the forehead, much like saluting a commanding officer. The motion for "ah" can be done with either hand. Depending on which hand is used, the impulse is passed either to the person directly to the right or left of the sender. Whichever way the fingers are pointing on the salute hand is the direction in which the impulse is passed. The player must say "Ah!" in a sharp, loud, staccato command simultaneously with the hand motion to create and collect the most energy for the group. Practice it a few times to make sure everyone is clear.

- The second sound is "so," and the motion for "so" is similar to the type of salute used with "ah," but the hand is brought to the stomach, with the thumb facing in. "So" is said in the same drill-sergeant-like manner, and as with "ah," the salute for "so" can be given with either hand. Whichever way the fingers are pointing is the direction the impulse is passed, directly to the person on the right or left. Again, practice it a few times.

- Now, the person receiving the "so" impulse must send it to someone across the circle (anyone except those immediately to that person's right or left). The sender does so by looking at a person directly in the eyes, clapping his palms together and pointing at that person with his fingertips, keeping his palms together. As he does this, he says, "Zoo!," with much gusto, sending the impulse across the circle to that person. Practice this sound and motion a few times.

- The person who receives the "zoo" impulse begins the pattern again, passing the impulse to the person on his/her right or left by saying "ah" with the proper salute.

- When players miss either a motion or the proper command, they are ceremoniously told they can no longer be a part of the circle. This is done by the remaining players putting a thumbs-up into the middle of the circle and saying, in an umpire-like manner, "You're out of the game!" while jerking their thumbs upward and outward from the circle. Once an ejected player moves outside the circle, the person who was to his/her right has 5 seconds to restart the game with an "ah."

- Now, the players who have been ejected from the game can still participate by becoming hecklers. Hecklers try to make other

players mess up by distracting them in clever ways. There are three rules to heckling: 1) hecklers cannot touch anyone, 2) they cannot yell in other players' ears, and 3) they cannot block other players' vision. The best hecklers are often quiet and creative. It helps to give examples of what might work. My personal favorite is the soft-rock radio DJ voice, "You are listening to light 100.5, and the sounds of the center of your head!"

- Another level can be added to this game after it has been determined that players can handle the three motions described so far. When someone passes a "Zoo" from across the circle, it can be rejected by putting both hands up in front of your face and exclaiming, "No." This sends the impulse straight back to the sender, who must begin the sequence over again with an "ah" and the proper salute.

Variations

- Changing the words to more obviously fit the actions makes this activity good for younger kids or some special-needs populations.

- Karl Rohnke coined the name of the game Ah, So, Ko! We think "zoo" is a better sound. You decide what works best for you. We have also had great success substituting with "High, Low, Yo!"

Whoosh, Wham, Whoa, Wow!

Contributor/History

Origin unknown.

Concept/Objective

This is a great energizer!

Props/Materials Needed/Preparation

No props needed.

Directions/Scenarios/Instructions

Whoosh, Wham, Whoa, Wow! is a simple game that is sure to help you gauge and assess the energy levels and playfulness of a group, as well as get the group fired up and energized! As you introduce this game, it is important that you really give it your all, give it your best energy, because this game is played with nothing that most people can actually see—Energy!

* Have the group members stand in a circle. Tell them that you all are about to play a game that has four distinct actions for the four words, "whoosh," "wham," "whoa," and "wow." As you begin to explain the game, reach into your pocket and pull out the invisible ball of energy you are going to be playing with. Begin with it being about the size of a shooter marble, or super ball. While explaining about the invisible ball, I begin moving my hands around, as if I were actually rolling the marble-sized

ball between my palms—gradually making the ball grow—
never touching my hands together. The more you do this, the
more you may actually feel the warm ball of energy growing in
your hands. Play with it! The more you do and the more you
feel it, the more your group will!

- Invite anyone who would like to take out their own invisible ball
of energy and play with it. Explain about energy and why it is
important to be aware of both our own energy and each other's.
Keep rolling the ball around and turning it over, as you would a
good snowball, until it grows to the size of a baseball or softball,
no larger than a small cantaloupe. If someone in the group has
a good ball going, invite him/her to share it with the group for
the activity. Have that person toss it to you and continue to keep
it going, rolling it in your hands as you explain the activity. Once
you have the ball of energy vibrating and alive and the group
members focused on it, teach them the actions for the words.

- Explain that the object of this activity is to pass the energy
around and through the group using the four words: whoosh,
wham, whoa, and wow. Begin with "whoosh." When you
pass the ball to the person directly on your left or right, say,
"Whoosh!" as you do so. Give it a try! Pass the ball all the way
around the circle until it comes back to you.

- Next introduce "Wham." "Wham" is used when you wish to
send the energy ball to someone across the circle from you,
to someone who is not on either your immediate left or right.
When you wham somebody, make sure you are directing the
pass right to them. Keep the size of the ball in mind as you
pass it, extending your arms out in front of you, as if making a
chest pass in a basketball game, while keeping your palms facing one another. This will help the energy retain its shape as it
flies across the circle to its intended recipient.

- The next action is "Whoa." I have seen "whoa" used a few different ways. It is beautiful in its duality! The "whoa" is played
to block a pass. While saying "whoa," place your hands in
front of you, palms facing out, and cross your arms into an
"X," blocking the pass. If "whoa" is played, the energy returns
to the passer, who tries passing it to someone else. Usually,

I set this up so that one may only "whoa" a "wham." If you are "whooshed," you must keep the energy moving by either "whooshing," or "whamming."

Understand that a "wham" can be a little intense for some. People who are a bit more reserved or inhibited can actually use "whoa" as a means of "Challenge by Choice."* We have, however, seen it used as playfully as the rest of the actions in the game. Usually, those who pick up on the playful use of "whoa" end up rubbing off on those who used it as an escape clause, and bring them along in the fun!

- The last action to introduce is my personal favorite. "Wow" is used when you are just so overcome with the amount of energy being sent around the group that you cannot contain yourself. Rather than pass it using "whoosh" or "wham," or send it back to someone with a "whoa," you may revel in the glory of that feeling by throwing your hands up over your head, jumping a little bit, and saying excitedly, "WOW!" The whole group then mimics your actions, saying "WOW!" Do and say "WOW!" as many times as you are moved to, and then pass the ball around some more with either a "whoosh" or a "wham!"

---

* "Challenge by Choice" is copyrighted by Project Adventure. This concept is used to describe the idea that people should feel that they have control of their adventure experience (Schoel, Prouty, & Radcliffe, 1989; Rohnke & Butler, 1995).

This game usually starts off with a few skeptics and cynics, but by the end of the activity everyone has gotten into it, has laughed, and is well, believe it or not... energized!

Variation

Our good friend Jodi Angus taught us another fun twist to this energizer. After the group gets the hang of it and really gets the energy moving around, you can introduce, "WOOOOO!" Anytime anyone says "Woooo," the entire group repeats it with great exuberance, moving around the circle franticly while swinging their arms over their heads and finding a new spot in the circle. A wacky and fun way to move to a different spot and meet a new neighbor!

Zip-Zap

Contributor/History

We believe this is a New Games Foundation original, though we learned it from Steve Ockerbloom at Renbrook Summer Adventure. This activity is also in *No Props* by Mark Collard.

Concept/Objective

Zip-Zap is a great, low-level energizer that engages groups both young and old. We have used this activity as a stand alone, or combined with the name game Bumpity, Bump, Bump (see Variations). Either way, people are sure to have fun and become energized and playful.

Props/Materials Needed/Preparation

No props needed.

Directions/Scenarios/Instructions

- Have the group stand in a circle. Begin by standing in the middle of the circle as you explain and demonstrate how to play, and start off as "it."

- As the person in the middle, it is your job to walk up to someone and very clearly indicate that you are choosing him/her. Make eye contact and clap your hands together in a two-handed point directly at the person with whom you want to play, and say loudly and clearly, "Zip!" (Use very clear and direct actions.) It is the job of the person who has been zipped to duck or crouch down.

- The two people standing on either side of the zipped person quickly become involved at this point. They turn to the zipped person, clap their hands together to point at that person, and say, "Zap!" They will end up pointing at either the person who was zipped, or to the person on the other side of the zipped person, if the person who was zipped is crouching down.

- The last person to react with the appropriate action now moves to the middle of the circle, becoming "it." The person in the middle who is "it" is also the judge and rules on the individual game of Zip-Zap played! The faster the action, the more fun the game becomes.

Variations

- Once the group picks up on how to play, the facilitator can step back into the middle and begin another round so that there are two "its." This definitely picks up the pace of the game! Depending on your group size, you may add one or two more people as "it;" however, it can get a bit out of control! Once

you step back in as the second "it," make sure you let everyone know that it would be unfair to "zip" a zapper already engaged in a Zip-Zap battle.

- This can also be combined with the name game Bumpity, Bump, Bump. Preface it by letting participants know that this is a name game, and they will need to introduce themselves to the person on their left and on their right. They will also need to know the name of the person in the middle as well as their own name. This always gets a laugh because, who doesn't know his/her own name? There is always someone who forgets his or her own name in this activity!

Bumpity, Bump, Bump starts out the same as Zip-Zap. Walk up to someone, clap your hands together in a point, and look directly into that person's eyes. Now say one of four things: "Left," "Right," "You," or "Me," followed quickly by "Bumpity, bump, bump!" (For example, "Left—Bumpity bump bump"). If the person you have pointed to can say the indicated name, (in this case, the name of the person on his/her left) before you finish saying "Bumpity, bump, bump," that person is safe, and you move on to the next poor unsuspecting person. If, however, you beat that person, or that person just doesn't know the answer or forgets his/her own name, you take that person's spot in the circle and that person becomes "it."

We have lots of fun combining these two games. They are both great as standalones, but to combine the two is lots of fun. It can set the stage for discussions on multitasking and the need to be able to shift gears or skills quickly in later activities.

After starting with the name game, Bumpity, Bump, Bump, we then ask participants to stick it in their back pocket, remembering it for later. We then introduce Zip-Zap and play many rounds of that before slipping back into the middle and walking up to someone to play Bumpity, Bump, Bump. This throws them off a bit, but we have found that groups love the combination of the two activities and it causes much laughter and good energy. Isn't that what it is all about?!

Evolution of Group Focus
Looking Back in Front of Us

3

A group will direct its collective focus, consciously or subconsciously, to the group leader, each other, or a combination of both. This is true when first coming together, or after having been formed as a team over time. The direction of this group focus, which is sometimes determined by the educator's style and intentions, has seen some changes over the last 40 years.

To illustrate this evolution, we will reflect on some adventure education movements and educators. Some have withstood the test of time and are still relevant to this day. Some have faded from the landscape. The trends from these movements and practitioners have informed and taught us and have guided us in our practices as reference points along the journey of our experience.

As a beginning point, let's take a look at the evolution of adventure education as a formal school-based program. We believe that this is a good place to start, because it will allow us to remember its history, as well as peek forward from there to the present day.

In 1971, Project Adventure was formed and implemented into the school-wide curriculum at Hamilton-Wenham High School, north of Boston, Massachusetts. Because of the uniqueness of the program, it spread quickly to some other area schools, courtesy of Karl Rohnke and a few of his cohorts. Those of us who have had the pleasure of interacting with Rohnke know that he works well as the visible leader of a group. His charisma, enthusiasm, and the gleam in his eye make it difficult to avert your attention elsewhere.

Essentially, Rohnke was the perfect person to be leading the advancement of this "new" type of learning. In those times, high school PE teachers were the visible authorities on learning in the

physical education classroom. This was especially true if adventure education activities were part of the curriculum. All eyes focused on the teachers first and their instructions were heeded. The activities that were being introduced were a little outside the mainstream for that time. They were often viewed as risky and a little kooky. Students generally felt that they had better pay attention to what the teachers were saying or they might get hurt.

Notice that the word "new" is in quotations in the previous paragraph. That is to indicate that although this type of learning may have been new in schools, it had been around long before that. A brief history lesson brings us backwards in time to the Outward Bound program. This was representative of a type of expedition-based learning upon which Project Adventure based many of its philosophies and teachings. Since much of that learning was wilderness based, the leader/teacher had to be very experienced and knowledgeable. The level of focus on them was very intense. They became almost revered and the info they had to teach was greatly sought after, if only as a way to stay safe while in the wilderness.

Look backwards even further. Outward Bound drew some of its influences from the military, where rank and the chain of command dictated a mandatory focus on your leaders. They taught you all you needed to know to survive in many of the situations you might encounter. Ropes courses were used for survival training and as fitness builders. An intentional element of fear was built into those learning situations. The military was and is very leader centered.

Moving forward from the birth of Project Adventure and the arrival of other groups that used similar teaching techniques, it is helpful to examine the tone of some of the teachings and philosophical underpinnings that were used in those days. We think it may help you see some of the subtle changes that have taken place.

Two important play-based education movements coexisted in the late 1970s. The New Games Foundation existed to create large events in cities and towns. It grew from a need for people to come together and to feel like they were making a difference at a time when our country was divided by war. People played cooperatively, experiencing the gains and benefits of that type of human interaction in a very organic way. The organization of the activities was very much leader directed and staged, but very participant centered in implementation. The social unrest in our country was an impetus for the cultural mainstream to accept this as a new way of recreation and socialization. Once the political focus shifted, the New Games Foundation seemed to fade from the landscape, their work completed, a job well done. Their ideas that fun is important and that a sense of belonging to something bigger than you is worthwhile remain a legacy that is still felt throughout the world.

Project Adventure, on the other hand, continued to gain momentum and some acceptance by schools as an alternative learning style. By the time *Cowstails and Cobras II* was published by Project Adventure (1989), Karl Rohnke was deeply entrenched as the face of the company, and indeed, of the adventure education movement, at least here on the east coast. Rohnke's "calculated abandon" led participants directly to him or other educational leaders like him as the focus of fun and learning.

Also important to note, is the first occurrence of the suggestions that group leaders who wanted to run these programs should lead reflective discussions after the activities so that the participants could learn from them. It was the last suggestion in *Cowstails and*

Cobras' pedagogical discussion and almost an afterthought. It was clearly leader centered and provided a point for comparison to current debriefing materials, which are more participant centered and participant driven.

The evolution of adventure education and experiential teaching continued throughout the 1980s as teachers and group leaders interjected "risk" activities into curricula to break up the comfort zones that people liked to exist within. These approaches were seen as the best way to cure boredom, celebrate change, and rise above the mundane. This approach resulted in educational leaders being viewed as specialists. Even though reflection and processing around these risk activities was becoming more common, the debriefing was still very leader directed.

In *Silver Bullets* (Rohnke, 1984), we finally had a reference to the goal of adventure education being that the relationship between the participants had some value and deserved some focus. Learning goal # 4 for adventure education activities is as follows: "To develop an increased joy in one's self and in being with others (p. 9)." It also said, "Instructors are not solemnly engaged in building confidence, social cohesion, and agility" (p. 9). This suggested that the instructor was responsible for the fun. So, at this point in time, we were still leader centered, but there was some recognition that fun was important. It was easy for us to move forward on the notion that fun would not happen if it weren't for interaction with the people around you.

As we progressed through the later years of the 1980s, the usefulness of reflective practices became more meaningful. As the art of facilitation began to take hold, educational leaders began to use processing tools to lead discussions after learning opportunities to try and make connections from the learning activities back to their everyday lives. As more group processing took place, this type of learning and teaching began to be seen as having a place in the pedagogical world.

Further evidence of this evolution of thought was seen in the development of adventure-based counseling as a new approach within the larger field of experiential education. Counselors and social

workers started to use adventure education to transfer gains from the group's training experience to other areas of life. This became an important role in the expansion of where the group might focus its attention. The participant plays a larger part in this process. So you can start to see the evolution toward participant-centered activity happening.

Let us fast forward to today's times. In the last few years, there have been an extensive number of books written and workshops given around what we call the soft skills of facilitation. Current best practices seek to help groups or teams move forward through the stages of group development. A great deal of techniques now exist to assist us in helping groups and teams become cohesive and effective, and process the experiences themselves. To be participant centered and participant driven is now the goal for most high-functioning groups. It should be noted that while this is a worthy goal for our groups and teams to aspire to, it takes skill and patience to make this a reality. There are many instances when leader-directed questioning is the most effective method to help group members transfer their learning to other areas of their lives. For both leader-centered and participant-centered debriefing to occur, it is essential that educators and facilitators spend as much time selecting possible debriefs as they do the activities used to illustrate lessons. We feel that these processing sessions become very important learnable moments because of the focus they require. Self-reflective skills are sharpened. This also allows the reflections to move toward being more participant driven.

The process that a person or a group follows as focus increases is similar to the path groups follow along any model of the experiential-learning cycle. As thoughts occur, they help to evaluate past knowledge in relation to new. The energy that comes from new thoughts stimulates an awareness of one's own locus of control. This awareness fuels the courage to make new choices. These choices lead to intentional physical actions that lead to new results, and the process begins anew. As an educator or facilitator of learning, this becomes a crucial process to learn as you relate thoughts from debriefing sessions back to this continuum of thoughts.

We can see that the direction of a group's focus has evolved from being leader centered to more participant centered. Why is this important? It tells us that we have a lot to learn from each other. It shows that how we perceive others and their actions has a direct effect on how we learn. In fact, fairly recent brain research indicates that we are learning from our environment all the time by merely watching and observing.

We will next share our knowledge about how mirror neurons work. These are something that we all have in our brain that help us learn as much by watching as we do by having a physical experience. This new knowledge of mirror neurons underscores how the evolution of group focus has shifted recently to include a little more learning from fellow group members and a little less from the facilitator, teacher, or leader. The interesting thing to note is that the shift is really imperceptible to the team members. As we gain more knowledge about this phenomenon, we may desire to shift our energy and affect toward encouraging learners to be more aware of their interpersonal interactions during group work and classroom time, as well as during less-structured learning opportunities.

The Mirror Neuron Party

4

We will say it again, as classroom teachers, facilitators, and leaders of learning, we need to be mindful of the energy and affect we bring to our classes and groups. This may be realized in deeper ways than we have ever really given thought to. It seems that most of us have these interesting little motor neurons at work in our brains called "mirror neurons," which pack a whole lot of functional fire power. Now, we are not brain scientists by any stretch of the imagination, let's set the record straight. But we do love to bounce ideas around and reflect a bit, and we have both become mildly—okay, completely—obsessed with these neural phenomena and how they relate to groups, group formation, and group focus.

Have you ever wondered why, at the end of a really close, exciting college basketball game, say during the month of March, as the clock ticks down the final seconds of the game and your team puts up a three pointer at the buzzer, you find yourself standing up in your living room with your arm extended in full follow-through as though you were taking the shot yourself? Why do we wince when watching someone else get hurt? Why do we well up with tears or even cry when watching a touching movie or television program? Have you ever noticed yourself squirming with the creeps as you watch a spider crawl up someone's leg? And who hasn't caught a yawn as it is passed, seemingly contagiously, throughout a room?

Now picture the groups you lead. Are there times when you, as the facilitator or teacher (who has both seen and participated in so many activities time and time again), have a physical reaction, flinching or wincing, as the group stumbles through the activity? I am sure many instances pop into your head. One that comes to mind for me involves an activity called "Trolleys." Trolleys is a classic team-building initiative involving 2 long, 4" x 4" wood boards

with 8 to 10 ropes coming up through the boards to use as hand holds. The basic idea is to have the group move, all together at the same time, from point A to point B, using the trolleys to walk on. This is how it might play out: The group members board the trolleys and get hold of the hand ropes. Someone, with the confidence that this is going to be easy, says something like, "Okay, left!" As several people try to move the left trolley, you involuntarily either feel like lifting or actually step and pull your left foot a little bit off the ground as if you were doing the activity yourself. This is an empathetic response, physically manifested due to the firing of mirror neurons in our brains.

The discovery of the mirror neurons happened a bit serendipitously. Giacomo Rizzolatti and Vittorio Gallese of the University of Parma discovered mirror neurons in 1995 while researching the firing of neurons in an area of the macaque monkeys' premotor cortex each time the monkeys reached for a bite of a peanut. The big surprise was that there was neural activity not only when the monkey was picking up the peanut and eating it but also when it observed a human perform the same action, even in a different context. It is still unclear when or how the actual "aha" moment appeared—the researchers themselves don't have a clear memory—though there are several versions of the story that lead to the same outcome. A favorite version relays the tale of a when Gallese entered the lab with an ice cream cone. As Gallese raised the cone to his mouth to eat, the monkeys, who still had electrodes connected to their inferior frontal cortexes, began to have all kinds of neural firings, just as they had while performing the very same action themselves with the peanuts. This discovery led to more research and to findings that human mirror neurons are smarter, more flexible, and far more evolved than those of monkeys, which speaks directly to the sophistication of humans' social abilities.

Mirror neurons are located in the frontal cortex and parietal lobule of the human brain. The discovery and research of mirror neurons has been one of the biggest breakthroughs in brain science research in the last 15 years.

One study, performed by Marco Iacoboni, another neuroscientist at the forefront of the research into mirror neurons, along with his colleagues at UCLA in 2003, had people's brains scanned using a magnetic resonance imager (MRI). Study participants were shown pictures of other humans making faces associated with various emotions—smiling (happy), frowning (sad), snarling (angry), mouth agape, eyes wide (surprised)—you get the picture. They were asked to imitate the faces they were shown. When looking at the happy face, the MRI revealed activity in the happy emotional part of the brain. The results were the same in the corresponding areas of the brain for angry or upset faces. The results were consistent, even when the participants were asked merely to observe the faces without imitation, which would indicate a reflective response, as if the participants were actually making the faces themselves. According to Iacoboni, mirror neurons can send messages to the limbic or emotional system in our brains. It is possible that these neurons help us tune in to each other's feelings. That's empathy.

One of my all-time favorite activities is Pipeline, an age-old activity where group members use pieces of PVC pipe to transfer a marble or ping-pong ball across a distance into a bucket where it makes the most wonderful "pluck" noise (see p. 119). In the process, the marble must never lose forward momentum nor be dropped or touched by anyone. This activity is perhaps one of the best il-

PHOTO BY MIKE GESSFORD

lustrations of what we affectionately refer to as a "mirror neuron party." The group struggles along beautifully for a while, learning by watching, learning by doing, trial and error. A few bouts with frustration usually lead to the formulations of plans, and eventually, small steps toward success. I can't begin to tell you how often we have seen groups get right to the very end, mere feet from the bucket, and drop the marble on the ground. The collective moans and groans and sighs are the same every time! When the group finally does make it to the end and get the object to its home, that "plunk" causes the biggest celebration!

Why does this activity come to mind more than others? I think it has something to do with mirror neurons and the collective experience. At one point or another during the activity, each participant had the marble in his/her tube and experienced what that felt like, both tactilely and emotionally. When the last move was made, even if one was not actively transferring the object to its goal, one was actually doing it in his/her mind at the same time. When that marble hit the bottom of the bucket there was this collective celebration that all could share; hence, the mirror neuron party.

Collective experiences like this are powerful because of the empathic responses. Next time you try this activity, pay attention to the group and how it progresses through this activity. That sound at the end always gets the same reaction. I have even gone as far as to play with this to see what reaction could be triggered by dropping the marble into the bucket later in the program. The group members paused for a moment and shared the memory, smiling and having that experience replayed in their minds at the same time; the mirror neuron after-party.

Why is all this brainiac talk useful? Let's look at how mirror neurons and empathetic response relate to the processing and reflection portion of our programming. Subtle physical mimicry of people's actions or gestures, if done in such a manner as to not draw conscious attention to it, allows for an empathetic response based on the shared physical experience. A recent experiment conducted at Nijmegen University in the Netherlands by a psychologist named Rick van Baaren had study participants view a series of advertisements and give their opinions about them.[*] During the observations, a research assistant would very subtly mimic the postures and arm and leg positions of half of the participants while they spoke about their opinions of the ads, being very careful not to be too obvious about it. A few moments later, the researcher would "accidentally" drop six pens on the floor. What the researchers found was most interesting. Those who were subtly mimicked during the interviews were two to three times more likely to help pick up the pens than those who were not mimicked at all. The researchers concluded that the mimicry increased goodwill toward the researcher in a very short amount of time. It also turns out that the participants' helpful and generous behaviors were not limited solely toward the researcher doing the mimicking but also toward people not directly involved in the mimicry situation, suggesting that the effects "are not simply due to increased liking for the mimicker, but are due to increased prosocial orientation in general."

---

[*] Van Baaren's research report from the study at Nijmegen is available at http://www.psych.yorku.ca/kawakami/documents/mimicry.pdf

There have been several other experiments conducted regarding subtle mimicry. The common thread is that participants who were mimicked in a good way, that is, subtly, without malicious intention, were more likely to have that positive, pleasurable social high that activates the areas of the brain involved in sensing reward: the mirror neuron ice cream social.

This is so important for us to keep in mind as teachers, counselors, and facilitators. Our affect has a direct effect on the group. Smiles and laughter are contagious. An awareness of the energy we bring to our groups can result in the best possible experiences, based on what they pick up consciously from one another and unconsciously from the nonverbal cues communicated by both the facilitator and the rest of the group members. Our understanding and use of the subtleties of body language and its effect on others can allow people around us to be more at ease because of the shared experiences.

It has long been known that proper activity sequencing is important for the overall success of our groups. Now we may have a deeper understanding of why certain warm-ups and icebreakers have the effect that they do. Take for example some age-old warm-ups such as Micro-Macro Wave Stretch (p. 113) or Snoopy vs. The Red Baron (p. 128). In both activities, we engage in mimicry, albeit overt and everyone is aware of it. It seems, however, that the over-all effect is the same—we mimic, we lead, we mimic some more, our bodies stretch and our minds and attitudes relax. People begin to open up and feel more comfortable with one another.

Let's also consider the icebreakers Instant Replay (p. 109) and King Frog (p. 111). Instant Replay always starts out a little bit uncomfortable. The object is for participants to introduce themselves with their name and a quick gesture or sign that represents them. Usually the first participant to go is a bit awkward, but once the group mimics that person and repeats his/her name, the ice has been broken. It becomes easier and easier for each subsequent group member as the introductions go around the circle. Now, that was a very generalized statement. Of course there are those who are more shy or more outgoing, those who are quicker to think creatively on their feet, and those who are more or less inhibited; but generally, the collective effect of the group seems to ease up a bit, to relax, to become more congenial.

Similarly, King Frog is an activity that involves an introduction (each person's animal name) and a corresponding motion to go along with the name. With King Frog, however, there is a bit more memorization involved. One needs to remember the other people's animal names and motions to be able to continue in the game successfully. I believe the overall effect is the same, at least regarding the mimicry and how our mirror neurons engage us in an empathetic shared experience, allowing us to let down our guards, to mellow in to our groove together as a group. The activity works; the ice cracks and we begin to catch glimpses into who we are under those layers of cool, who we are a bit deeper down. When we do get to the more in-depth group work, we have laid a firm bedrock of good feelings to build upon as we move through the stages of group development and team cohesion.

See if this sounds familiar. You are early in your program, perhaps an hour into the day, and the group has been playing along fairly well. You have played some name games, done some icebreakers, and just finished playing a warm-up or icebreaker. There is a small group, say two or three people, who are clearly on their own trip.

Maybe they arrived as a clique, maybe something happened on the bus ride in; whatever the case, these two or three characters are hell-bent on sabotaging the rest of the group. They play along, but are clearly not on the same page as the rest of the group. They are constantly disruptive, break the rules, and/or talk about something completely unrelated to what the group is discussing. We refer to these folks as the "mirror neuron party poopers."

If not dealt with appropriately, these people are likely to drag the rest of the group down and detract from the overall focus. It is absolutely necessary to reel these people in, to have the group mind override the few who are not there yet. Now, this may be far easier said than done! Who hasn't had the participant who becomes defensive and oppositional? It is not fun, though these definitely can be powerful learning opportunities for everyone in-volved. The key is to allow the person to change his/her behavior and be rewarded for it. Opportunities can be given to test the new information and behaviors within the group, letting the person know that s/he is valued for this new way of thinking and ap-proaching the rest of the group.

How do we do this? Just as it is important for us, as facilitators of learning, to be aware of the energy and affect we bring to our groups and the effect it has upon the participants, we also need to be aware of the energy and affect of the individual group members. There has long been discussion and theories taught in the fields of counseling, education, and experiential education about how to properly sequence activities and programs by using a variety of assessment tools and sequencing methods. Whichever models you use, it is always important to constantly reassess where your group or class is along the stages of the group-development continuum. There are some important questions to ask yourself along the way. Is the activity or lesson plan appropriate for the group's current developmental stage? How is the group behaving? Will the plan of action be helpful or harmful for the group based on its behavior? How does the group appear energetically? Is the activity or sequence appropriate for the setting or location of the program or class? Understanding the answers to these simple but helpful questions will allow you to switch gears, if you need to, and to keep the group moving in the right direction. With careful sequencing and a good toolkit of activities, both active and reflective, we can create powerful learning opportunities with potential for many transformative experiences.

I feel that we, as "people people," who self-select the types of professions that allow us to work deeply with others, have a natural understanding and inclination to be empathetic. That is, we are already masters of the mirror neurons, or "mirror neuron party emcees." It is our job to make sure the party is rocking in the right way in order to enable our groups to tap into each other's greatest potential through focus.

Individual Focus

Nothingness is Good

Building on the brief overview given in chapter 4 of the mirror neurons that reside within all of our brains, this chapter investigates how individuals may achieve better control over their own focusing powers. Some of the reasons why we don't take the time to observe very well will also be examined. There are various approaches we can use to change our mindsets and ways of observing. We will begin by speaking about the importance of spending quality time with one's self, not only to practice being open but to also allow for the occasion of being open to occur with more ease and therefore give greater value to that practice.

In a July, 2008 newsletter, a team-building company called The Table Group, offered some insight into the importance and possibilities of individual focus. The CEO, Patrick Lencioni, suggested in his article, "The Art of Pondering," that as leaders of groups, whether of family, work, or otherwise, we need to take the time to ponder and reflect on our organizations. He observed that often, we don't take the time to sit and spend time in undistracted thought. The author suggested that some of the reason for this is an adrenaline addiction, the compulsion we feel to be constantly in motion, busy, and productive. He also stated that another reason pondering is difficult has to do with influence that the media has on society. We are constantly encouraged to stay connected at all times. A few newspaper articles have said emergency rooms are seeing an increase of injuries to people who have fallen while walking and text messaging at the same time. Maybe that is the natural extension of being able to walk and talk at the same time, but we don't think so. We often see evidence during our daily work that people have unconsciously convinced themselves that by staying busy, they can avoid having to face the problems of the various groups and teams they belong to.

To address the situation, Lencioni suggested we need to do two things. First, as leaders, we must admit that we underponder and that might be why our groups underachieve. Secondly, we should build time into our schedule to ponder and tell the people in our groups and organizations that we are going to do so. This will help them accept that you are not just sitting around wasting time. We believe that before you schedule time for yourself to ponder and reflect, you need to become aware of the best setting or style of activity that allows you to open your mind and focus on your thoughts. Try various places and times for uninterrupted thinking. We imagine one's pondering place may be quite different from another's because of the many divergent ways people find calm. Additionally, where and how we ponder is very closely related to our dominant learning styles.

I often have instances of greater insight when engaged in some type of solitary activity. I can get lost in the rhythm of repetitive motion while hiking or bike riding. I feel my mind empty and become clearest when involved in an activity kinesthetically. In this state, I can start to enter a place where thoughts and ideas tend to just flow more freely. Sport psychologists such as W. Timothy Gallwey (1974) in his book, *The Inner Game of Tennis*, often refer to an inner place like this that is known as "the zone." This is a seemingly elevated state of consciousness where good thoughts just seem to flow, instincts take over, and the explanation as to why things occur isn't often obvious, nor does it need to be. It is described as a state where very little thinking occurs at all, existing totally in the present.

It is important to know the best way we become open to our thoughts, or how we enter our zone. While we determine our best pondering places, it is just as important to know what situations to avoid. Some places or surroundings lead us toward negative self-talk, and we become trapped in negative cycles of thoughts. We enter a familiar situation and our thoughts quickly lean toward the negative because of past experience. It is our mirror neurons firing and leading us to believe we are likely to repeat this experience. The fight-or-flight syndrome kicks into high gear. Our experience tells us that a certain outcome is most likely. Therefore, we tend to look for that result. However, it doesn't have to be that way. If we are open to what might be possible, instead of what has happened previously, the usual result can be turned around, making it possible for new outcomes to occur.

In *Extraordinary Golf*, Fred Shoemaker (1996) urges us to become a "master of the possible." We appreciate the possibilities of this phrase. He says this is possible through improving our ability to concentrate. Shoemaker defines concentration as "The ability to focus your attention on that which you choose for as long as you choose." As a professional golf teacher and instructor, he has made a study of the swing thoughts of many of his students over a long period of time. His conclusions lead him to believe that even though we are trying to focus on just one thing, there are many thoughts that we actually jump to, based on our past experience. He also notes that there are minute gaps in between the thoughts where other influences can creep in. It is these gaps that we need to focus on closing. You have a choice. The gaps can either be filled with chatter, worry, doubts, and judgments or nothing. Concentration is, in a sense, nothing; and that nothing can help your focus.

Those who have played golf might recognize the following scenario. You are in the middle of an average round, you have hit some

memorable shots and some forgettable shots. On a par three, your tee shot ends up in a green-side bunker. There is a small pond on the other side of the green, which is sloping away from you. The voices in your head start to suggest that if you run your shot past the flagstick, your ball will end up in the drink on the other side. So, you take a few practice swings, carefully thinking about all the techniques you want to do well. There is a running conversation with the voices in your head. Negative images linger because of the possible consequences of a poorly hit shot. After a few more test swings, you address the ball and start your backswing. You can feel that your swing is going to end up being nothing like the way you practiced it. You end up chili dipping the shot. The ball doesn't even get out of the sand trap and rolls back to your feet. This is very frustrating, since your shots in the practice bunker before your round were consistently good. What you could have done is thank the voices in your head for their contribution, but put them aside. Replace their swing thoughts with the fact that you may just hit one of the best bunker shots you ever have. Often, this positive imagery will be enough to remove the self-interference, help you relax, and enable you to make a great swing at the ball. The result close to the one you wanted and envisioned is much more likely to occur.

The lesson to be learned from this is that this act of intentionally being open to the good outcome, with good intentions, puts you in a place where the power of your focused mind can take over.

An excerpt from *Open to Outcome* by Micah Jacobson and Mari Ruddy (2004) helps us learn where our focus may go when we seem to lose it.

> *Ask yourself, "What are you noticing right now?" For instance, if I was leading a reflection right now, many of you would be focused on me, but some people might still be thinking about the activity we just did or even a previous debriefing. Others might be noticing different aspects of the room or maybe a headache or nagging body pain. You may even notice that as I ran through the list, your attention shifted through the different things I called out, finally resting on that nagging body pain. Our attention is critical. Every moment of our life we are processing a huge amount of stimulation. Most of it is unremarkable and gets little attention.*

That is why it is so important to know how you can get to a place where the distractions are minimal, so as to best facilitate focusing and pondering.

In order to combat those distractions, we need to set ourselves up for success by practicing the skill of putting ourselves in places that are conducive to deep thinking, physically and emotionally. We also need to practice the skill of opening ourselves, so that the increased focus will allow the productive thoughts we are seeking to enter our consciousness.

In addition to increased focus leading to better access to the thoughts that help you formulate new ideas, there is another long-term benefit. Easier access to your thoughts also creates a feeling that the thoughts that occur in this manner indeed have important value. This increased value will result in strengthening our bond with the natural world, which consists of nature and the other people we share it with. When people and groups value this organic world, created by some higher power from which we all came and exist in, we tighten our ties to this world. We are encouraged to be more active stewards of the environment and of each other. The man-made world that we increasingly surround ourselves with each day is a reality for us; however, it is important for people and groups to maintain a relationship with the natural world. Feeling

this organic connection allows our minds to gain the benefits of being open and aware of any new ideas that may surface from it.

One way we have found to best take advantage of the connection to nature and other people is through a technique called "quiet watching." In his book, *The Leader Who Is Hardly Known*, Steven Simpson (2003) describes quiet watching as a meditation technique that is designed to prolong individual focus. He suggests that nature is often the best place to practice quiet watching. You can do so by deeply focusing on a large object such as a cloud, a mountain, a pond, or even a campfire for at least 10 minutes or more. When thoughts drift to things like job or family issues, the meditator realizes that focus has momentarily been interrupted and returns his or her attention back to the object. As you practice this centering activity, you should realize greater lengths in between lapses.

Another technique that Simpson refers to in *The Leader Who Is Hardly Known* is that of "walking meditation." This is similar to the repetitive activity I spoke of earlier that seems to help open my mind. Although, the hiking or biking is not completely the same, because one of my main goals for hiking or biking is to get exercise. The goal of walking meditation, in this case, is not exercise nor in-

ner enlightenment. It is openness. Stated another way, it is developing the rare skill of sauntering. Sauntering is roving and wandering with a purpose, but having that purpose be the pleasure of roving and wandering. The point of getting into nature in such a way is to be one with nature, where there is no distinction between the seer and the seen. It is to be open to the possibilities.

Because the great outdoors is not always available to us when our time to ponder is scheduled (or needed!), we have developed an indoor activity called Washer Pendulum, which has been helpful in achieving a state of elevated focus. This exercise is accomplished by deeply focusing your individual energy on an object. It helps to develop the skill of blocking out extraneous input from your environment and to concentrate solely on one thing at a time. This exercise is described on the following pages.

Washer Pendulum

Contributor/History

This particular activity developed from a chance meeting at the 2006 AEE International Conference in Minneapolis. The concept of using a washer tied onto a string to help show common energy was introduced to us by Becky Disciacca, a teacher at the Horace Mann School in New Milford, Connecticut.

Concept/Objective

The goal is to be able to control the washer and its movements while remaining as still as you can by focusing all your energy down the string to the washer. With great focus, you should be able to make the washer swing from side to side, from front to back, and in a clockwise and counter-clockwise motion.

Props/Materials Needed/Preparation

You need washers that are about the size of a dime (5/16") and thin cotton string (nylon string is harder to work with when tying the knots). Tie a foot-long piece of string to a washer, using two half hitches cinched up tight. Tie a simple overhand in the other end of the string to keep it from unraveling. Trim the ends of the strings close to the knots as long ragged ends can be distracting.

Directions/Instructions/Scenarios

- Sit in a chair or on the floor with your elbows resting on your knees. Press the washer-free end of the string to your forehead using the index finger from each hand. This two-finger method, combined with your elbows on your knees, will help to stabilize your whole shoulder girdle and upper body. Let the washer pendulum hang down in front of you.

- The goal is to be able to control the washer and its movements. With great focus, you should be able to make the washer swing from side to side, from front to back and swing in a clockwise and counter-clockwise motion. Once you have practiced these motions, you should be able to do them in a random order. It will take a few seconds when switching from one direction to another. Keep your focus.

- Next, try making it stop completely.

Variations

- Once you have mastered these movements and want to move to the next level, try it with a partner. Hold the string by pressing your foreheads together. Be aware that when working with a partner, directions are sometimes opposite. For example, when you declare that you are going to work together to make the washer move in a clockwise motion, the person who says that should make a spiraling motion under the washer with her

index finger so both partners are clear as to which direction that is.

- Have all participants move their washer pendulums in the same direction at the same time.

Debriefs

Notice the level of concentration you need in order to get this to work. This is the feeling you are trying to achieve when you are being open or becoming the "master of the possible."

6

Group Focus

That's Ubuntu!

As we move the discussion from the individual to the group, let us revisit two phrases mentioned earlier that seem to be central themes for the groups that we work with: "individual responsibility" and "mutual accountability." In group work, it quickly becomes evident that we cannot act solely for ourselves if we are to have a positive collective experience. Groups are comprised of people who are more and less capable than we are at performing certain tasks or processes. This realization can creep up when the task-oriented people, or those who are overly enthusiastic, jump right into an activity without regard for other group members' thoughts or ideas about how to approach the activity as a group. These are opportunities for us to ask our group members to examine themselves, individually and collectively, regarding these concepts. When we are being individually responsible, taking care of ourselves, and doing the very best we can at whatever it is we are supposed to be doing, then we can be mutually accountable to the group. This accountability involves checking in, offering help, holding one another up to the standards set forth, and giving the best of ourselves to our groups. It is these two concepts that seem to connect the focus of the individual to the group. If one is not focused, than how can one be a focused member of something bigger than one's self?

There are many times in my life that I can think back to and attribute success solely to what I have done by myself, for myself, or for someone else, but accomplished just by me, alone. These are excellent moments for self-reflection and acknowledgment of individual accomplishment, and although individuals create many great things by themselves, we do not, for the most part, live as hermits, isolated from the rest of humanity. We live in families and in societies comprised of cities and towns, and even those who live by themselves, fairly isolated, at times need to interact with and rely upon other people. As a species, humans are wired to be social beings, and we are actually able to become better than we already are through other people.

While the successes we have as individuals are wonderful and can help us to feel good and increase our own self-efficacy, what good are they if they aren't shared with someone else? As I think about the individual successes I have had, most, if not all, really involve other people, either directly or indirectly.

As facilitators of learning, we seldom work with just one person, unless we are doing some one-to-one tutoring or instruction. We work with groups of people who arrive with their own individual experiences of successes and failure, their own perspectives about the world and about other people, their own expectations for what they will bring to the day, as well as their expectations for the rest of the group and the facilitator. They also arrive, at times, as intact groups who have already experienced collective successes and failures, and have preconceived notions about the others in their groups based on their prior experiences with these people. It is our job to frame learning opportunities that will touch upon every individual in our groups. In order to do this, we must be open to everyone's experience and everyone's learning styles. We must be careful not to allow our biases or preferred learning styles to dominate the framework for the possible learning experiences we provide.

One of the most important variables to consider when working with groups is creating a space that is safe and welcoming for learning. Now this does not mean to forego the perceived risk portion of the programming that we all love and has drawn many of us to the fields of adventure and experiential education, that aspect of our programming will be better received, by and large, through proper sequencing. Nor is this concept limited to those who work in "risky" environments. It applies to classroom teachers, counselors, social workers, camp counselors, or anyone whose aim is to set up a nurturing learning environment.

Simply stated, be hospitable. Consider yourselves stewards for learning. No matter who the group is, where the members come from, or what outcomes they are hoping to achieve through working with us, people desire and need to be treated with kindness and respect—with hospitality. Treat your groups as you would guests in your home. By doing this you are creating a safe space where people feel comfortable. The more comfortable people are initially, the more they are going to be willing to open up to the possibilities. They will be more likely to engage in the seemingly risky or less-comfortable activities as the group progresses through the stages of group development. The age-old concept of hospitality is described in detail in a recent book for people in the field of experiential education and group facilitation, *Teams for a New Generation* (Robinson & Rose, 2007).

There is a South African term from the Bantu language that beautifully encompasses the concepts of hospitality and how people can and should coexist. Ubuntu, simply explained, means, a person is a person through other people. Or, put even more simply, I am because we are, or even more simply, me, we. Ubuntu is a concept brilliantly described by Bishop Desmond Tutu in the "Semester at Sea" speech he gave in the spring of 2007.

> *In our country we've got something called Ubuntu. When I want to praise you, I say this person has Ubuntu. Because in our culture there is no such thing as a solitary individual, we say a person is a person through other persons; that we belong in the bundle of life. And I want you to be all you can be; because that's the only way I can be all I can be. I need you! I need you to be you so that I can be me. The only way we can be human is together! The only way we can be free is together! The only way we can ever be secure is together! The only way we can ever be free... is together. That is the logic of God's creation.* (Bishop Desmond Tutu, 2007)

The Boston Celtics recently embraced Ubuntu as their team concept and mantra, using it to replace the age-old, "One, two, three, Celtics" when coming out of a huddle. They went on to win the NBA title for the first time in 22 years, stressing the importance of collective success over individual achievement.

The concept and idea of Ubuntu is precisely what we as group facilitators are trying to get our groups to recognize and achieve. Think about your groups for a minute. High-performing groups, those that accomplish the tasks and initiative problems we present to them efficiently and effectively, are essentially practicing Ubuntu. They have utilized one another to the best of everyone's abilities, recognizing and utilizing the resources within the group. Everyone has been involved in some way, shape, or form, and everyone feels the same success, the same sense of accomplishment.

Many of our groups really embrace the concept and teachings of Ubuntu, even using it as a mantra. Group members point out when someone within their group is exhibiting qualities that demonstrate Ubuntu by saying, "That's Ubuntu," followed by the rest of the group saying, "I am because we are." These have been very powerful moments indeed. Groups remember this concept. It is simple and makes so much sense. Plus, it is just plain old fun to say, Ubuntu. If the entire world could embrace this concept and start living with Ubuntu, we could truly turn some things around. By embedding the concepts of Ubuntu and hospitality into our programming, we will ultimately create a safe and vital learning environment.

We talked earlier about the importance of being inclusive of all learning styles as well. If we are cognizant of the divergent styles of learning and the multiple intelligences that individuals possess, we can impact more people. Think back to when you were in school for a minute. Was there ever a time you just didn't get it? Or, if you were one of the lucky kids who always got it, I am sure you remember kids who seemed intelligent enough, but seemed to get lost, or just tuned out, or become distracted or distracting to others. We now know, thanks to Howard Gardner, that there are many types of intelligence and that, while most of us have a dominant learning style, we can and do possess many, if not all, of the multiple intelligences. Gardner's (1983) theory of multiple intelligences has gained widespread popularity and acceptance in the field of education over the last two decades, and while we do not wish to go into it too deeply here, we thought it was important enough to mention. We encourage you as facilitators of learning to understand it and incorporate it into your programming.

According to Gardner, there are eight major categories of intelligence: bodily-kinesthetic, interpersonal, verbal-linguistic, logical-mathematical, naturalistic, intrapersonal, visual-spatial, and musical. The more we use and openly discuss strengths and limitations in learning, using learning styles and multiple intelligences as the focus, the more aware we become, not just of our own strengths and areas that need improvement but also those of our group members. This new knowledge is empowering to groups because it enables the group members to understand not only how each person learns best but also why they may be better suited to perform a particular role or task within their groups.

Perhaps the least touched upon of the intelligences is music. Rhythm and music, particularly drumming and especially group drumming can have a profound focusing quality. Drumming has been used in cultures the world over. (Imagine someone stumbling over a hollow log thousands of years ago and discovering it had a really good tone!) Group drumming has many profound benefits, including focus. Using biofeedback, research has shown that the drumbeat can reduce stress by altering the brain's wave patterns, increasing alpha waves, which are light, meditative brainwaves. Talk about a healthy alternative to pharmaceuticals! How

great would it be if rather than prescribing medications and treatments for stress, doctors gave you a prescription for a djembe drum with weekly follow-ups at the local drum circle? Now that is good medicine!

One of the biggest misperceptions of group drumming is that one has to be a musician to play drums. This is simply not true! Think back to when we were children, uninhibited, curious, and how we would bang or tap on things, exploring our rhythmic creativity and sounds. When I was about 18 years old, I had the pleasure of attending a drum workshop given by the legendary Nigerian master drummer Babatunde Olatunji in Santa Cruz, California. Olatunji had a great catchphrase that has stuck with me (and probably every drummer he played with over the years). "If you can say it, you can play it." This is so simple and so true.

Start by saying your name, first and last, and take note of the meter of how your name is said. Now, as you say your name, tap it out at the same time alternating your hands with each tap. It's that simple. We have used this in our programming with great success. We've even used words, phrases, or concepts from the group norms or "Full Value Commitments,"* drumming them at the

---

* A concept developed by Project Adventure. See *Islands of Healing* (1988) by J. Schoel, D. Prouty, & P. Radcliffe.

same time, to begin the groove. Once people realize that they can play what they can say, they are empowered to try new things, to follow along on new beats and new rhythms. There isn't anything more powerful than a group of people deep in a groove together. Drumming can be almost hypnotizing when groups get to that point. A common physical and rhythmical experience can create deep focus. The "world music mirror neuron party!"

Another fun and engaging rhythmic activity we use as a means of discussing learning styles and multiple intelligences is one we have fondly begun to call Pringles Stomp (see p. 65). The beauty of Pringles Stomp is that it begins as an individual focusing activity, but as it progresses, it becomes a group focuser. We all start with varying levels of comfort in the rhythm and performance piece of the activity and approach learning it in different ways. As you watch this activity, you can see the focus gradually shift. I usually take as much time as the group needs before getting to the passing of the cans portion of the show. Sometimes, however, people will actually do better once the pressure to pass the can is on. In which case, I will move it along, throwing out the old adage, "Fake it 'til you make it." This usually kicks it up a notch, but stress can be a great focuser.

The shift in focus truly is amazing! What began as "How am I going to learn this?" has shifted to, "We are jamming!" The beat goes on with the rhythm pumping out faster and faster, a few stumbles here and there, but by and large, the group is jamming! "Me" has become "we" and we are having a serious musical mirror neuron party! If the group is really cooking, I turn up the tempo, slowly, beat by beat, faster and faster, until someone ends up feeling like Lucille Ball in the episode that took place in the chocolate factory on the television classic, I Love Lucy! This is usually a great way to stop—exhilarated from the jam, focused as a group from creating a common rhythm and operating as a well-oiled machine, passing the cans in rhythm, and laughing at the chaotic ending of a massive pileup on some poor soul who couldn't keep up.

Take into consideration that you may want to save the I Love Lucy ending for a group you know will be able to deal with it. I have had

some people end up extremely frustrated, and of course that is not the goal at all. However, this can be a great focuser for the group that is clicking along and has a good sense of humor.

Have you ever had that group that just couldn't get its sillies out? You know, the gigglers, the nervous laughers, or the kids who are just sharing a private joke or kidding around on the side? We have had great success refocusing these situations with a simple and fun activity called Laughing Symphony (see p. 70).

We have found that shared common physical activities can have a positive effect on group focus. Activities that provide everyone with the same experience allow groups to eliminate outside distracters and narrow their focus to a lower common denominator.

Another method we like to use to bring a group into focus is Bull Ring (see p. 73), during which everyone is essentially doing the same physical motion. There are a few reasons why shared common physical activity is helpful for refocusing.

First of all, everyone should be feeling pretty much the same physical forces in their bodies. That makes establishing and using a common language much easier. Participants will have a better understanding of the words being used by other group members, since they are all operating from the same base of physical sensation.

Second, they are all focusing on a common object. This helps make the problem objective because the object is inanimate, making it impersonal. Focusing on other people sometimes leads to bickering and off-task conversation, thus affecting the efficiency and effectiveness of the group.

If the group is successful with Bull Ring, then we might use a variation called Write Together (see p. 132). There are other choices in the alternate activity section in chapter 11 that may accomplish these same objectives.

Pringles® Stomp

Contributor/History

This is a variation on an old rhythmic activity of origin unknown. We learned it from a former colleague, Shalon Paul. We use empty single-serving-size cans of Pringles® because of their ideal size and dual tonal qualities. We affectionately call this Pringles Stomp because it reminded us of the now-famous group of performers seen on Broadway and in their own videos and national performances, *Stomp!*

Concept/Objective

This activity illustrates the shifts in focus from that of the individuals to those of the group. The objective is for everyone to learn the rhythmic pattern and be able to perform it simultaneously—keeping the rhythm pattern going, passing the can at the end of the pattern, and then receiving a new can to repeat and continue the pattern. Look for the video demonstration of this activity on our Web site, www.focusyourlocus.com.

Props/Materials Needed/Preparation

You need one can for each participant. While we use empty cans of Pringles, any old small cans with lids may be used. We have also used cups of various sizes. You will want to stay away from using glass, as this activity does involve banging and we do not wish to add any element of danger!

Directions/Scenarios/Instructions

Those with musical intelligence will love this activity and for those who may think they are not at all musical, you can remind them of the old playground favorite, "Mike and Justin up in a tree k-i-s-s-i-n-g." That is the entire pattern, and remember, from earlier in the chapter, Babatunde Olatunji said, "If you can say it, you can play it!" We are all far more musical than we give ourselves credit for!

- Have the group sit in a circle. This can be done either on the floor or at a table; the group will need to be able to reach the cans comfortably in order to do this correctly.

- Demonstrate the rhythm. I usually have them watch and listen to me do the whole thing first. (After this initial performance, you can sometimes see by the looks on peoples faces who is excited and thinks this will be fun; who is a bit perplexed, yet intrigued; and who is completely out of his comfort zone and thinks, "There is no way I am going to be able to learn that!" Validate each feeling and reassure the group members that this can be done and that you will help them learn it!)

- Now, break the rhythm down and teach it to the group in two manageable parts. Once the group members have gotten through the first part, which they usually do pretty quickly, we move on to the second part. If you refer to the verbal-linguistic write-up, this has you starting with the can already moved over about one foot to the right. Practice this as much as the group needs to before you put it all together. Remember, this is no professional performance piece and that you may encourage people to "Fake it until they make it!"

Simply by virtue of you being there teaching it in person, you are attending to the interpersonal intelligence, as well as the visual-spatial intelligence. At the end of this write-up you will find three different approaches we have found helpful for people with divergent learning styles. The write-up for the verbal-linguistic learner spells it out exactly, but completely takes the soul out of the jam. It is probably the way most people in the group will appreciate learning it and, once you get into the rhythm, you can adapt it and say something like this in order for the words to fit the rhythm, "Clap-

clap, tap-tap-tap, clap, grab, place-clap, scoop, up, down, grab, smack, place." You will also find it written up in musical notation, for the mathematical learners, as well as in picture form, for those who are visually-spatially intelligent.

Variations

We have used this activity in many different ways and for different reasons.

- Once the group masters the initial rhythm patterns, you can add the reverse round. Reverse is just as it sounds. Someone says, "Reverse!" and the cans now need to be passed in the opposite direction (to the left, or clockwise). This can present all kinds of new dynamics, as now the left hand becomes the primary hand for grabbing the can.

- Have group members decorate their cans with markers, stickers, or whatever. Invite them to put words or phrases in the cans describing what they will need in order to get the full value out of their time with the group. As the cans are passed, periodically call, "Stop!" and ask one of the participants to open the can she has and read what is inside. Another way to incorporate the intelligences into "Full Value Contract" creation!

- Another variation, similar to the one above, is based on an old activity called Fears in a Hat. This is designed to allow the group members to begin to support one another's fears or concerns anonymously by writing them down on slips of paper and placing them into and drawing them out of a hat. For the Pringles Stomp version, simply have the group members place their written fears or concerns into their undecorated can (if anonymity is the name of the game!). Take time to process what is read with the group each time, and they will begin to notice how the group can support and address their fears and concerns without ever having to know whose was whose.

PHOTOS BY JARRAD McGLAMERY

Pringles Stomp (Verbal-Linguistic Write-Up)

Part One

Clap—Clap

Tap Tap Tap

Clap—Grab Top With Right Hand

Move 1 inch to the Right and Place Down on Table (Lid-Side Up)

Part Two

Clap—Reverse Grab (Thumb Down)

Rotate Clockwise Up, Tap Bottom of Can on Downward-Facing
   Palm of Left Hand

Place Can (Lid-Side Down) Down

Rotate Clockwise Up

Grab Top With Left Hand

Smack Table in Front of You With Right Open Palm

Cross Left Hand Holding Can Over Right Arm

Pass Can and Place in Front of Person on Your Right

Repeat

Pringles Stomp (Mathematical Intelligence Musical Notation)

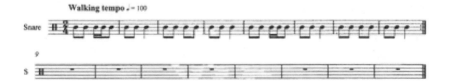

Look for the video demonstration of this activity on our Web site,
www.focusyourlocus.com.

Laughing Symphony

Contributor/History

This is a variation on an activity that we learned from Roy Charette at a Connecticut Challenge Course Professionals conference in 2003. His original activity was Emotional Symphony with different sections performing agreed-upon qualities of various emotions. Laughing Symphony was something I came up with one day when I had a group who simply could not get its sillies out.

Concept/Objective

Laughing Symphony is an opportunity for groups to either get their sillies out or, if they are too serious, have a chance to get silly. Either way, laughter can be a powerful tool for a teachable moment.

The focusing quality of this activity is nothing to scoff at either! I suppose we can giggle at the fact that the outcome of this silly-sounding symphony can be one of focus and calm.

Props/Materials Needed/Preparation

No props needed for this one, though I have used a small stick like the baton of an orchestra conductor for effect.

Directions/Scenarios/Instructions

- Have the group members circle-up, standing fairly close together, but not touching.

- Ask participants if they know what a symphony is, and briefly discuss how musicians know when to start and stop playing their instruments. They will invariably tell you about the conductor.

- At this point, let the group members know that they are, in fact, going to become part of a symphony orchestra, though this is no ordinary orchestra of woodwinds and strings. For this orchestra, the only instruments needed are laughs. Teach the group your signs for start and stop. I usually throw in a sign for crescendo and decrescendo (louder and softer)—be creative. Think about the conductors you have seen throughout your experience and then take it to the next level of silliness. The more the group sees your willingness to let it all hang out and get silly, the more it will buy in.

- I sometimes have the group warm up with hums and quiet giggles much the way an orchestra tunes up before its performance. I then tap my conductor's baton (stick) on my invisible music stand and make sure all eyes are on me. Upon the initial signal to begin, I too commence in loud, ridiculous, over-the-top laughter, which gives the participants the idea of what we're doing, as well as permission (to those who need it) to be as zany as they wish.

- After a minute or so, signal the group members to stop, give them good strokes for playing along, and encourage them to work on the ending. Usually the first round ends with a few stray giggles and laughs, so talk to them about the importance of ending at precisely the same time, just as the greatest orchestras do. This is one of the ways this activity becomes a focuser. Much like the activity Photo Finish, the object is to end at exactly the same time.

- Do the activity again. Take notice of the amount of focus that is happening now. Even those who aren't as exuberant in their laughter are still engaged and ready to be successful by ending at the same exact time.

The other reason Laughing Symphony seems to work well as a focuser is because when we laugh, even when we are faking it, we actually reduce the levels of stress hormones such as cortisol, epinephrine (adrenaline), dopamine, and growth hormone. Laughter increases the levels of health-enhancing hormones like endorphins and neurotransmitters. It increases the number of antibody cells while enhancing the effectiveness of T-cells responsible for a strong immune system. Laughter really is good medicine!

Bull Ring

Contributor/History

We originally saw this activity demonstrated by Jim Cain. It comes from his book, *Teamwork & Teamplay*.

Concept/Objective

The challenge is to have participants hold the ends of a strings that are attached to a central metal ring. The group then uses this apparatus to pick a small ball off a pedestal, carry the ball through a series of obstacles, and place the ball onto another pedestal.

Props/Materials Needed/Preparation

The bull ring is made from a 1-inch metal ring and 6 pieces of string, about 20-feet long. We prefer masonry line as it comes off the roll easily and is very colorful. (The ring and masonry line are available at most hardware stores.) Burn the ends of the strings after cutting to avoid fraying. To attach the strings to the ring, simply wrap the string around the ring, so that equal lengths are hanging off of it. Then tie the string as close to the ring as possible with a double overhand knot. That should leave you with 12 ten-foot strings coming from 6 knots tied to the bull ring. Variations to the structure can include the size of the ring, the size of the ball, and the size of the stand that the ball starts on originally. The finished bull ring along with the ball and pedestal can easily be transported in an old tennis ball can.

Set the stage by placing the ring (with the strings attached) around the pedestal in the center of the room, and fanning the string out from the center. Place the ball on top of the pedestal.

Directions/Scenarios/Instructions

As a focusing progression, we like to use three simple initiatives to help groups all feel similar physical sensations.

- Ask the group members to pick up their end of the string. Explain that the object is to apply some tension to the strings, slide the ring up the pedestal, pick up the ball, raise it to waist height. They then return the ball to the pedestal and let the ring slide down to the floor without disrupting the pedestal.

- The second objective is exactly the same, except that once the ball is at waist height, the group must rotate 360 degrees around the center pedestal before returning the ball and ring to the pedestal.

- The third step in the progression is to do another simple raise and lower, but this time all group members should only have one eye open the whole time.

Debriefs

The usual observations from the group are related to feeling tension from the other group members. There can be conversations about good tension versus bad tension, which can lead to discussions about how conflict is handled in the group. Is conflict kept issue driven, or does it start to become personality driven?

Another outcome that people notice is the change in perspective when you have only one eye open. Depth perception changes and participants become reliant on others to provide them with the information needed to do their part to help the whole group be successful at completing the task. This can lead to a discussion about communication styles as well as assertiveness in asking for what you need to do your job well.

The important experience to review is how it felt, physically and emotionally, when the group was all pulling at the same time. Notice how you felt inside when the ball was first lifted. How did you feel when you realized that you may have to change the amount of tension you provide for the group to reach its goal? How did you feel when other group members' tension didn't seem to match your own? These reactions to change and stress are all good things to be aware of, so that when you do find yourself losing focus, you have an awareness of your tendencies. That will help you to adjust in order to do your part to the best of your ability.

7

Leading Versus Facilitating
A Slice of Humble Pie

There are several words that mean similar things and are often used interchangeably to describe people who are responsible for the learning journey of a group. Because they are thought of as synonyms, they are often misused. Let's consider the terms teacher, instructor, leader, and facilitator. I believe there are important distinctions to make between these roles and words. Understanding the difference can help you employ different modes of communication and display corresponding levels of energy as the group's learning journey continues. For our intents and purposes, this is what we will use as a basis for the following discussion:

A **teacher** creates stimuli at a level that encourages learners to improve. A teacher will find a way to make content become motivating and relevant to the learner.

An **instructor** informs the learner of a standard so that it can be repeated back.

A **leader** moves the learner from point A to point B at the learner's request. The learning outcome is known to both the leader and to the learner. Usually, the learner is following the leader.

A **facilitator** moves the learner from point A to point B, but the method and destination are unknown. The learning outcome is not known to the facilitator or to the learner before they begin. A level of trust must be present. Occasionally, the learner may be followed by the facilitator as the journey continues.

As one who is responsible for the learning of a group, the energy you give off should match your job responsibilities and the potential learning outcomes of the group you are in charge of. You may be required to use any one or a combination of these various roles in order to be fully effective. Being aware of the level of energy you give off might help you more effectively change roles as the group progresses through its work and learning. As a facilitator, ask yourself the following question: While my input might lead to a successful solution and lessen or eliminate some conflict, will my input diminish the accomplishment of the group?

The central question should be: Am I helping the group learn its own lessons or am I trying to teach it my lessons? As long as safety concerns aren't compromised, the choices should come from the group as much as possible. Additionally, what works for a group at one point in time might not be appropriate at another time because the group dynamic and/or knowledge has changed through experience. Although your motives may be to help the group work toward its goal, ask yourself, "Did they really need my help?" Often, the answer is no.

A few years back, Justin and I had an important learning moment as we facilitated a relatively simple team initiative. I know it must be important, because we often refer back to it. Upon reflection, it was a true test for us as facilitators, and for the students as group members.

Let me tell the story of the Gengras Center's 45-minute line up by height. A group of 10 special-education students were going through an adventure education sequence as part of their PE class. They were ready for some group problem solving and given the seemingly simple initiative of arranging themselves in a line by height. They could speak to each other. Past experiences told us that a group that size could accomplish this in about 3 minutes or less, without talking. However, this group had many challenges; we were just not immediately aware of how all these challenges may be manifested during this activity.

These students were high-school age. One girl, Mary, was in a wheelchair because of a debilitating muscular condition. To the other students' point of view, Mary was the shortest because she was sitting, so she was parked at the end of the line and not really consulted again. (Interestingly enough, when she had assistance to stand, she was actually one of the tallest in the group.) Up to this time, it had been a challenge for the group members to think about how they could include Mary in their activities.

The group members began rearranging themselves amid much discussion, as well as some disagreement. As time wore on, Justin and I kept looking at each other and smiling. We could not comprehend some of the logic that was being offered. It was hard to be silent. Some of the students held rigid thoughts about personal height that related to their own self-image, but was projected onto their classmates as well. There were statements such as "I'm not shorter than you!" "I'm 19 and you're 16, so I have to be taller than you." This led to a lot of going back and forth and rearranging. Realities clashed. Time ticked on.

Whenever the class wanted to check its progress, we gave feedback using musical notes on a scale. Other than that, we said nothing. As we traveled down the row of students, we would sing a musical

PHOTO BY MIKE GESSFORD

note, higher or lower than the one previous, so students could figure out where the line might need adjusting.

When students felt they had another idea to offer, they would step out of line, turn around, and address the rest of the group. It was obvious that the concept of the initiative was difficult for some to grasp. However, some could definitely understand the task, and all of the students worked cooperatively. After some successes and some failures, frustration set in. As facilitators, we desperately wanted to offer them some help that might lead to a quicker solution. However, because they continued to work and stay focused on the solution, we opted to try and stay flexible, not to say anything, and to see where this would ultimately end up. We had to ask ourselves the question, "Is speaking up and offering advice what is most important at this time?" It is amazing to watch the paths that groups can take, left to their own devices.

After about 40 minutes, we noticed that fewer group members were involved, and the initiative had evolved into a power struggle between a few members of the group. In an effort to again involve the whole group, we simply asked, "Mary, what do you think?" Mary lifted her head and perked up as somebody wheeled her out in front of the group. You could see her thinking. The rest of the group stood silently as they watched Mary contemplate. After 15 seconds or so, Mary said, "You belong here, you belong there, and you two need to switch places." It took all of about 30 seconds. The group complied with Mary's directives. We did the musical test and the notes progressed higher with each student. They had accomplished the task 45 minutes later.

You can imagine the debrief we had from that sequence of events. It was rich with lessons about including everyone, listening to and respecting all ideas, perseverance, perspective, etc. They all agreed that "A good idea doesn't care who has it."

The students were pleased that they had finally accomplished the task, and thankful for Mary's abilities to see the solution. When we asked Mary how she was able to line up her classmates so quickly, she replied that when she was wheeled out of line, she was able to look at the lines made by the bricks on the wall behind the class. That made comparing their heights easy. This was an "aha" moment for the rest of the group, especially those who tended to be "know-it-alls." They were thinking linearly, concerned about what their final place in line would mean about their self-image. Mary was thinking systematically, using the relationship (physically) between her classmates and the lines from the bricks on the wall to compare heights and realign people.

This experience became a critical point in our education as facilitators. Patience paid off with so many teachable and learnable moments. The process was not one we had imagined, but because we let it develop at its own speed, it turned out to be a crucial moment for the group's development, and therefore very reinforcing to our experience as well.

Your ability to help the group understand what happened during the activity by leading an effective debrief may be more useful as a resource to the group. Often, the debrief can be about the group's level of involvement versus its level of commitment. It is kind of like the bacon-and-eggs breakfast. The chicken is involved, but the pig is committed.

As facilitators, it is our job to create a hospitable space where team members can enter as friends, not enemies. Then we must let them go through their processes and progress through the stages of group development.

Those processes and stages have been described in many ways. M. Scott Peck (1998) referred to them as psuedo-community, chaos, emptiness, and true community. Similar stages of group development have been referred to by Bruce Tuckman (1965) as forming, storming, norming, performing, and transforming. The five functions of a cohesive team have been labeled trust, positive conflict, commitment, accountability, and results.

All of these stages or continuums operate around the ability to have participants sift through the remarkable amount of input, data, or "disturbance" that they face all the time. This is where the ability to focus and block out what is unimportant becomes crucial in each of the stages. It is only then that you can properly reflect and continue moving forward. As teachers, instructors, leaders, and facilitators it is our job to create the space, supply the motivation, and guide the transfer of new knowledge and concepts back to the larger areas of people's lives, whether that be in their individual circumstances or amidst the group they are a part of. Keith King explains this point well:

The act of learning is the result of reflection upon experience. Having an experience does not necessarily result in learning. You have to reflect on it. The purpose of learning is to gain something new and to put that new skill or information to the test of usefulness. In order to learn, one must be willing to risk exposing one's self to new things, be willing to test the validity of old things in relation to the new, and be willing to form new conclusions. I believe that to adventure is to risk exposing one's self to an unknown outcome. Therefore to learn is to venture into the unknown. To learn is to adventure! (King, 2004)

Lighter Than Air

We have almost reached the end of our program. The group has ridden the proverbial roller coaster of emotions and dynamics and stages of group development. We have regained the focus of the few individuals who were hesitant to fully engage in the group process, and now our group is performing at a relatively high level. Where do we go now?

We have found that once groups begin to achieve collective successes and are consistently performing well with the challenges presented to them, it is important to help them fully understand why this is happening and how to continue their successes. We often view failures as our greatest opportunities for teachable moments. It is just as important, if not more so, to utilize the positives and successes of the group members to further the understanding of why and how they have accomplished what they have, and why and how that can relate to the rest of their lives. These realizations can help them put all the pieces together, completing the experiential learning cycle puzzle.

It is often during these moments that we use an activity called Levitation, to help illustrate the collective power of the focused group (see p. 84). This activity is about the participants, and the collective power they share, and also about what to focus on.

Caution: The reaction to the Levitation is often one of excitement and awe. Groups love to talk about this; however, we encourage you to use caution in how you debrief this activity. Because of the powerful impact and because of people's various belief systems, we have found it is not appropriate to play with any mystical or magical metaphor when using this activity. Some participants will tune out, or become turned off, feeling that this may contradict their beliefs.

We have found that the best way to discuss this is by briefly explaining why it works, as described in the activity write-up, and perhaps relating it to Ubuntu. Then move the discussion back to how they can take the information about the collective power they cocreate back to their day-to-day lives and make more amazing things happen; things that can and will make a real difference. Levitation is a great conversation starter for discussions about community organizing and delegation of responsibility, as well as how to use the vision or mission of the group as the focus, rather than the task. If everyone is on the same page of what those are, and can focus on that, the tasks to carry out the mission and vision of the group become secondary and, therefore, maybe even "lighter than air."

Levitation

Contributor/History

Origin unknown. This is actually an old party trick that is often called Party Levitation. I learned this version after hours during a stay at an Adventure-Based Counseling training at Project Adventure in Beverly, Massachusetts.

Concept/Objective

The concept and objective is to demonstrate the collective power of a focused group, and change the focus from the task to the group.

Props/Materials Needed/Preparation

You will need a chair. A primer on proper spotting would also be helpful if you haven't already instructed the group in how to best do that yet.

Directions/Scenarios/Instructions

Remember when you were a kid and you'd spend the night out at a friend's house with a bunch of other kids? Or maybe at summer camp someone would suggest, "Let's do stiff as a board, light as a feather." One kid laid as flat and stiff as possible and the other four kids were supposed to lift that kid up effortlessly, using only two fingers on each hand, as though they were levitating him. Never worked, did it? Well, it can and it does. We were just missing the main ingredient: focus, on the same thing, at the same time.

We use this version of Levitation after processing a problem-solving activity, or as a closing.

- Invite the group members to circle-up and tell them that you would like to levitate someone as a way to demonstrate the collective power of their focused group. Explain that you will need a volunteer to be levitated and three volunteers to help levitate this person, using only two fingers each.

- Have a volunteer sit upright (in an armless chair) with arms at his sides and legs in a 90-degree angle, feet flat on the floor. To achieve the maximum reaction, pick a volunteer who is fairly good sized. If the person is too small, the reaction won't be as astounding.

- The three other volunteers assume the lifting position. Ask who would like to lift at the armpits and who would like to lift at the knee pits. It may be good, at this point, to check in with the person who will be levitated to make sure he will be comfortable being touched in these areas. "Are you ticklish?" usually gets a good laugh. Once everyone has decided who will lift where and is assured that the person being levitated is not going to giggle himself out of the chair, you are ready for the next step.

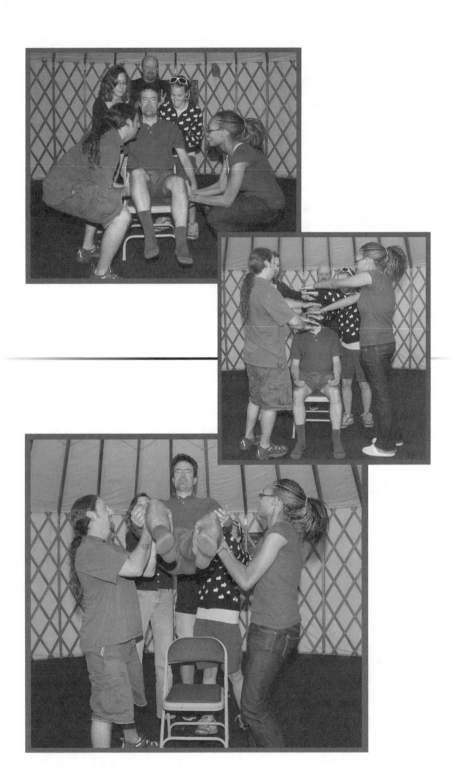

- Have the lifters assume the "James Bond" or "Charlie's Angels" position: legs spread, knees slightly bent, hands clasped together with the index fingers pointing out and the thumbs pointing upward. Make sure the person being lifted is also in the proper position: sitting upright, relaxed, but not limp, arms at sides, and legs bent at the knees in about a 90 degree angle, with feet flat on the floor.

- Once everyone is in position, tell the group that on the count of three, we are going to lift this person (use his name!) out of the chair, lighter than air. Now count, "One, two, three... lighter than air." Chances are, this first time, the lifters will struggle mightily, and the person in the chair will be jostled about a bit. However, the person probably won't be lifted out of the chair lighter than air. There will be giggling and skepticism, but don't give up yet!

- Shrug it off, and tell them, "Okay, okay, not quite lighter than air... yet!" Have them gather around the person in the chair, in the same places they were before. This time, place your right hand, palm facing down over the levitatee, in front of his face, at just about nose level. Ask the person on your left to place his open right hand, also palm facing down, above your right hand, leaving about an inch of space between your hands, so they are not touching. Ask the person on his left to do the same with their right hand, making sure to leave space between the hands. Finally have the fourth person do the same with her right hand. Now repeat this process, stacking left hands above the right hands, again making sure to leave about an inch of space.

- Tell the group to "focus on the tower of hands, and notice the feeling that is beginning to happen in the space between the hands." Have the group members move their hands in small sideways circles to "stir up the energy," again making sure not to touch hands, but allowing the energy to flow through them. I often describe it as "a warm, fuzzy band of energy that is flowing between our hands." Check in with all of the lifters and make sure they are feeling it. They will.

- Once they all acknowledge it, tell them, "Not now, but in a minute, when I say so, we will remove our hands in the exact opposite order of how we put them on, one at a time, taking with us the feeling of the energy we have just created. We will resume the lifting position, and on the count of three, we will lift so and so out of the chair, lighter than air." Check in again to make sure everyone is ready. Instruct the removal of the left hands, one at a time, then the rights, resume the lifting position, and count "One, two, three... lighter than air." This is always amazing. The levitators and the person being levitated will be amazed. The amount of effort exerted on the this try is significantly, if not drastically reduced.

Something to Think About: This activity has blown some minds! We have actually seen people let go of the person they are levitating out of sheer amazement, so spotting is very important. Have your cofacilitator and the group members not actively engaged in the levitation spotting. We have also been, as mentioned earlier in the book, accused of using voodoo! We assure the group members that this is absolutely not the case, just a beautiful example of the collective power of their focused group.

Without a doubt you will be asked how this is possible. We believe that it is truly the power of focused energy and people becoming one with each other. Hey! That's Ubuntu! On the first attempt, although everyone was lifting on the same three count, somewhere inside their own heads, they may have been counting their own three count. They may have been thinking, "I can't lift this person with two fingers!" This is entirely because of self-doubt, individualism, and "me" versus "we" thinking.

In the second attempt, the process of creating the tower of hands focused all of the attention on that, rather than on the task of lifting the person, changing the focus from the individual to the group. Shared vision and shared physical experience create synergy. Focusing on the tower of hands and on the energy that flows through and between those creating it, rather than focusing on the task at hand (lifting), allows the group to do amazing things.

Accessing Our Thoughts
The Usefulness of Focus

9

We end with a discussion of understanding why focus is both powerful and useful on a personal level as well as a group level. An understanding of the power of focused individuals and groups and how to redirect that focus is a very useful tool to guide groups through the stages of group development. If facilitators can get their groups comfortable with the approach that participants must learn from each other and with each other, then they should be able to successfully navigate their groups onto a higher level of functioning.

Both children and adults sometimes have difficulty navigating the uncertainties of group and team development. For children, one reason is that they have a tendency to be very connected to the electronic world. Being children, they tend to believe what they hear there as the truth. Being able to focus enables their own innate tools for critical thinking to be used to examine new information. This focus will not only help them gain access to their own original thoughts but also place value on them as worthy and meaningful as well. This greater sense of self-worth will enable them to become innovators and thinkers of the future. Many adults are developing an "urgency addiction"—a need to know everything as soon as it happens. New technology seems to make this easier all the time. People talk about multitasking, or the new term, "time slicing." This refers to the ability to do multiple tasks at once. However, I believe that the longest you can really focus on a task, before your mind wanders to something else, is from 30 seconds to a minute. Therefore, if people are convinced that they can multitask, I would suggest that their individual focus is split up between each of the jobs they are trying to accomplish. It is impossible to give more than 100% to everything, especially if you are doing them at the same time. One conclusion you could draw is that the quality of work from both tasks will be less than the best, since their focus is split. This practice of not focusing all your concentration on the one task or the problem at hand may lead to poorer results for you. An even greater consequence is that it affects the team or group you are functioning in. Plus, if you are basing outcomes and evaluations of your actions from just one minute or less of thinking about a task at a time, you might not be taking the time to consider the long-range impact of your decision on others. You only sense the immediate impact your results will have. This is another consequence to the urgency addiction we have created in our society. The ability to achieve and sustain focus or get it back to a sharper state will allow group leaders to then concentrate on raising the focused power of a group.

This ability to achieve and sustain focus may be addressed through the terms "efficiency" and "effectiveness." We often use an efficiency and effectiveness scale (see *A Teachable Moment* by Cain, Cummings & Stanchfield, 2008) in debriefing activities. This helps group members actually see where other participants rate the group's position on the scale. We define efficiency as "The ability of the group to complete a task in a timely manner, with minimal 'off task' conversation or effort." We define effectiveness as "the ability of the group to accomplish a job successfully, correctly, and without mistakes or errors." Used together, as described in *A Teachable Moment*, these paint a pretty vivid picture of how the group views itself at a particular point in time.

In order to harness the focused power of the group, it might require us to look at collective learning in a different way. In chapter 2 of *Teams For A New Generation*, authors Greg Robinson and Mark Rose *(2007)* discuss the three polarities that are inherent within team dynamics. These are the individual versus the team, action versus reflection, and change versus stability. It is these polarities that leaders must be aware of and try to balance in order to lead the team through the stage of storming. In thinking about team dynamics, it seems that we tend to strive toward one end of the continuum with each of these polarities. If we can accept the idea that there should be a balance between the ends of the polarities, we may well be on the way to creating leaders and facilitators that can handle the focused power of the group; facilitators who can lead their teams through that ever-important stage of storming, so that they don't enter into a world of irreparable dysfunction.

Consider the first polarity of the individual versus the team. When teams are forming, the focus seems to be toward the team end of the first polarity. There is a priority on finding where everyone fits, establishing cohesion, boundaries, goals, and so on. Often, an individual may view this polarity as an either/or choice. An effective leader will try to keep the group near the center of this continuum, so as to avoid groupthink, mediocrity, and loss of accountability.

Regarding the second polarity, when action becomes more important, a leader will have to deal with hasty decisions and repeating mistakes. When reflection is emphasized to the exclusion of action, the results may be paralysis by analysis. Reflection should be the beginning and the end of good group dynamics. Increased patience for both ends of this polarity must be facilitated for the group.

The last polarity that exists in team dynamics is change versus stability. Traditionally, the stability end of the continuum is emphasized more. Rules, goals, roles, and other things can make the complicated side of team dynamics become a little clearer. Additionally, without these constructs, higher-order thinking and behaviors such as collaboration would not be probable. We, as humans, are in a constant state of change, but change is intimidating to us because it requires us to ease our grasp on facts that we think to be true. Yet, it is the ability to adapt and change that allows teams to truly move toward the next great idea or performance.

There are two tools we have used effectively in helping groups deal with change. By doing so, it enables them to cocreate the next great idea. There is a phrase called "Yes, and..." and a conflict-resolution tool named "Communologue."

"Yes, and..." is from the book *Open To Outcome* by Micah Jacobson and Mari Ruddy. It is a tool that should be placed into your everyday conversations to replace the phrases of "Yes, but..." and "No, but..." We suggest that you do an experiment. Go through a day observing your conversations with others and listening to the dialogue between other people. See how many times you can catch the two phrases being used. Although it may not be intentional, these phrases essentially block any forward momentum the conversation may have been generating. It devalues the idea that preceded it and demeans the person who stated it.

"Yes, and..." however, keeps the conversation moving forward and allows continued momentum to build toward the next great idea. "Yes" doesn't necessarily mean that I agree with you, although it could. In this case, it means that I have heard you, and I recognize that what you just said was true for you at that time. Using the "and..." allows you to reply in a way that encourages conversation. Try it, and I'll be surprised if you don't notice a difference in the tones and directions of your conversations.

Another tool we use to help our groups focus when they need to manage change and uncertainty is a conflict-resolution tool called Communologue.[*] Communologue requires participants to listen deeply and use the techniques of mirroring, compassionate validation, and clarification to turn any power struggle or conflict from a debate into a community dialogue.

You can employ whatever tool you are comfortable using in these instances of conflict. We think the ones we have mentioned here are useful because they give us a structure to work through conflict. They use active listening skills to refocus people and groups when emotions are running high. Having systems such as these to fall back on tend to slow the process down, dissipate the emotions that arise with conflict, and enable us to truly hear one another. This allows mutual respect to be present, which helps us to work together to find a solution to the problem that got us here in the first place.

---

[*] Justin and Mike learned about Communologue at a facilitator's training on November 11 and 19, 2007 with Allan Schiffer, a psychologist in West Hartford, CT. For more information go to www.imagopeaceproject.org.

Attention Getters

Can You Hear Me Now?

10

Sometimes, as facilitators of learning, we find the need to quickly focus our group on what needs to be done or said next—to bring our group in line with the moment. We may need to give further instructions, relay some new, useful information, or start an activity debrief. It could be one of those teachable moments that we feel the pressing need to take advantage of immediately.

We would like to share some quick attention getters that we have found useful over the course of our experiences. This is not an exhaustive list, but it includes some of our favorites. They may stimulate your brain and spark an idea about how you could adapt a current practice to be used in this way. A lot of this list was taken from an online discussion of facilitators at www.ropesonline.org.

From James Bennett:
"Clap once if you can hear me."
Wait for a response.
"Clap twice if you can hear me."
Wait for a response.
(Continue until you have the group's attention.)
After doing this the first time, have the group set a goal of how few claps it will take the next time.

"Simon says raise your hands."
"Simon says put your hands on your hips."
"Simon says put your hands on your mouth."
"If you can hear the sound of my voice, raise your hand."
"If you can hear the sound of my voice, place your hand on your head."

From Jen Steinmetz:
Start a rhythmic clap. They will join in when they hear it. It becomes a bit of an energizer as well.

Have group members come up with and agree on a method they will use to get each other's attention.

Teach this to your group. "When I say 'All right' you answer with 'Okay!' When I say 'Okay,' you answer with 'All right.'"

From Donald Taylor:
Ask group members if they already have an effective method for letting you know they are ready to move on. Build it into their mindset.

From Frank Palmisano, Jr.:
Raise your hand and just stand there until people follow along and someone asks why. Tell them that you were trying to get their attention. Ask, "Is there a more preferable method you would like to use?"

From Bruce Lund:
In a classroom setting, use a rain-stick. When you turn it over, small beads come tumbling down. It is quiet, yet effective.

From Christopher Yucho:
Use a squeaky dog toy.

"Please take your upper lip and connect it to your lower lip."

"And a hush fell over the crowd." They respond with "hushhh!"

Chimes or bells.

Counting backward to zero.

From Michael Ohl:
"Look at what I'm doing right now." Then redirect them.

From Ken Tashoff:
Use Buzz Rings (Gyro Rings) to get their attention.

More Locus-Focusing Fun

11

There are many activities that we have used over the years to accomplish a certain amount of focus with individuals, groups, or a combination of the two. We share these in this chapter, so that you can take a look, use them, and determine if they would be as suitable for your bag of tricks as they have been for ours.

A Single Drop of Water

Contributor/History

From *Raptor and Other Team Building Activities* by Sam Sikes and *Teambuilding Puzzles* by Mike Anderson, Jim Cain, Tom Heck, and Chris Cavert.

Concept/Objective
Here is a challenge that is good at demonstrating the power of the focused group. It explores the fact that we can probably all do more than we think we can.

Props/Materials Needed/Preparation

You will need a penny, an eye dropper (available at drug stores), a glass of water, and a paper towel for clean up.

Directions/Scenarios/Instructions

- Explain that the challenge is to place as many drops of water on the head of a penny (coin) as possible.

- Before starting, let each member of the group estimate the total number of drops s/he believes will fit. Write down their guesstimates and compare them to the actual number of drops used.

Debriefs

We sometimes underestimate our own capacity. Just as this penny can hold more drops than is often estimated, so can we accomplish more than we believe. It teaches the importance of not underestimating your potential when setting goals. This activity can also lead to a great debrief on surface tension and the metaphors that come with that. Try other international coins, or a different liquid, such as soda or orange juice. Mix ingredients with water that will alter the surface tension, such as laundry detergent.

The Clock

Contributor/History

This activity came from the original *Cowstails and Cobras* by Karl Rohnke. It falls under the category of shared common physical activity, like Bull Ring.

Concept/Objective

The object of this activity is to complete a common task, as a group, as quickly as you can.

Props/Materials Needed/Preparation

A timing device is the only prop needed. Enough space is needed for group members to form a circle as they hold hands, with some room for moving about. Proper footwear for running and stopping is also a consideration to keep the participants safer.

Directions/Scenarios/Instructions

- Instruct the group to stand in a circle, facing the center. Have everyone join hands.

- Explain that when you give the signal "go," everyone will run as fast as they can in one full clockwise rotation around the circle. When they reach that point, they stop, change directions, and run back the other way to where they started.

As the facilitator/referee of this activity, you have two duties. First, wherever you stand next to the circle, that person standing in front of you will mark where a full rotation is to be counted. When that person returns to you after the first rotation, that is when the group needs to change directions. When they return the second time, the clock stops. Yes, that is your other job during this activity, to act as official timer.

Debrief

Help the participants to brainstorm possible verbal reminders they can give each other. Help to frame a discussion about strengths and weaknesses of group members, and possible helpful strategies and techniques for changing directions. Also, this is a great goal-setting activity that can illustrate how we often underestimate our abilities when we are part of a group. Ask if they noticed what their reaction to this stress was. When did they feel most comfortable? How about least comfortable? Are they becoming comfortable with being uncomfortable?

The Clock
(Webbing Adaptation)

Contributor/History

We learned this activity while we were working at Renbrook
Summer Adventure in West Hartford, Connecticut.

Concept/Objective

It is a stand-still variation of the old group initiative, The Clock
from *Cowstails and Cobras* by Karl Rohnke. The objective is to pass
the water knot (see below) that ties the webbing into a raccoon
circle all the way around the group circle, reverse directions, and
pass it back the other way. It is a timed event.

Props/Preparation

You need a piece of webbing that is tied together with a water knot
to make a circle. A typical raccoon circle, which is 15 feet of 1-inch
webbing with the ends tied together in a water knot, works well for
a group of 10 to 12 people. A water knot is a retraceable overhand
knot (see Figure 11.1 below). The ends of the webbing are tied together so they will not slip. You can adjust your webbing length
from the knot.

Figure 11.1

Directions/Scenarios

- Have everyone stand in a circle, facing the center, and holding the webbing in their hands. The water knot should be in plain sight, located in front of the facilitator, who is also the time-keeper for the activity.

- When the facilitator says "Go," the group must pass the knot around the circle, with the webbing sliding through everyone's hands as it travels. Once the knot travels a full revolution and arrives back in front of the facilitator, the group reverses direction and slides it around in the opposite way, until it gets back to the start/finish line in front of the timer once again. At that point the clock is stopped.

Debriefs

Possible debriefs include goal setting for the group, common language, coordination of physical efforts, the distractions that arise during the activity, and what each person focused on as the water knot traveled.

Deeply Rooted

Contributor/History

Origin unknown. An exceptional player and dear old friend of ours, Chip Stotler, introduced this activity to us.

Concept/Objective

This activity is all about deep focus.

Props/Materials Needed/Preparation

No props needed.

Directions/Scenarios/Instructions

- Ask someone to help you demonstrate the power of focus. Have the person stand with feet about shoulder-width apart, arms rigid and straight down on the sides, and hands clenched into fists. The goal is for this person to be lifted by two other volunteers who will flank the person on either side. Before any-one attempts this, have a brief discussion about the power of focus and the power of intention.

- For the initial lift, remind the lifters to use proper body mechanics, bending at the knees, keeping their fingers interlaced, creating a basket with their hands with which to lift the person by his or her clinched fist. I usually do the first lift as a straight-forward lift, giving no suggestions for the person who is being lifted. This shows that the person can in fact be lifted. The lifters should not lift this person too high, probably only 4 to 6 inches off the ground, and then return him/her to the ground safely.

• After the initial lift, ask the lifters to step away from the one being lifted. Now ask the person who was lifted to close his/her eyes and listen to a guided visualization. Say something like this:

"Picture yourself as a tree. Not just any tree, but the tallest, healthiest, strongest tree you can think of. See your trunk, bark thick and strong, stretching up, way up to boughs and branches, thick and strong, alive with the foliage that produces the freshest air to breathe... vibrant... alive... strong. Notice the sky behind the leaves, clear blue, accenting your leaves, green... strong... alive. Now visualize the nutrients from your leaves feeding you, giving you strength from the very top of your canopy all the way down, deep down to your roots. Feel the weight and warmth of the sun as it beats down on you. Feel the warmth of the sun running deep through the roots that anchor you to the earth. Feel the cool, rich soil, heavy with minerals, that surrounds your root system, deep down into the earth, keeping you deeply rooted to the ground. Now picture yourself, deeply rooted to the ground... deeply rooted to the ground..."

At this point, indicate to the lifters that they should try lifting the person again. Tell the person they are trying to lift to resist their lifting by remaining deeply rooted.

Most of the time, the lifters will not be able to lift the person after the visualization. If they are able to, often they will report that it was much harder than the first time. Play with this one. Help the person being lifted to really see him/herself as that deeply rooted tree. The people who are lifting have also tuned into the visualization and have had the same mental picture painted for them as well. This plants a seed, so to speak, that they are now trying to lift a tree that is very deeply rooted, a seemingly impossible task.

This activity always seems to empower the person who became deeply rooted. It can spark conversations about with whom the locus of control resides. Those who perceive an external locus of control can really have awakenings with activities like this, their locus focused.

Helium Stick

Contributor/History

We found this activity in two of Karl Rohnke's activity books. It is in *FUNN Stuff, Volume IV*, and *FUNN 'n Games*. He actually states that someone else deserves the credit for this initiative, but he isn't sure who that is.

Concept/Objective

Very simply, the object of the activity is for group members to lower the stick to the ground using only their fingers, without any group member ever losing physical contact.

Warning: This activity can be very frustrating. It is best used as a refocuser with a group that is already intact and has a history of being able to deal with conflict successfully.

Props/Materials

Lightweight tent pole (rigid or flexible) or other lightweight rod about 8- to 12-feet long. The longer the pole, the more participants needed, the harder the problem is to solve. Also, you can increase the level of challenge by placing 2 washers or round key rings on the ends of the pole.

Directions/Scenarios

• Have group members line up in two rows, facing each other, an arm's-length apart. Introduce the Helium Stick—a long, thin, light rod. Ask participants to bend their elbows 90 degrees. Their index fingers should be pointed straight ahead at the group members across from them, with their thumbs pointing down to the ground, inside the last three curled fingers of each hand. All of the extended pointer fingers should then be situated side by side.

- Lay the Helium Stick down on their fingers. Before you let go, have the group adjust finger heights until the Helium Stick is parallel to the ground and everyone's index fingers are touching the stick. Restate the objective of the activity. The important caveat: Each person's fingers must be in contact with the Helium Stick at all times. Pinching or grabbing the pole in not allowed. It must rest on top of fingers and hands must stay oriented to the ground as they were when the stick was placed on top of the index fingers.

Possible facilitator story line:

> *Organizations create mission statements to be a guiding force. A good mission statement focuses everyone's attention on the core essence of a business or organization, enabling it to make decisions and take actions that are directly aligned with their core values. For this next challenge, your group will have a simple mission: To lower this stick to the*

ground better than ANYONE in the world.

Have the group repeat the mission a couple of times.

Reiterate to the group that if anyone's finger is caught not touching the Helium Stick, the task will be restarted. Let the task begin....

Warning: Particularly in the early stages, the Helium Stick has a habit of mysteriously floating up rather than coming down, causing much laughter and/or frustration. A bit of clever humoring can help (e.g., act surprised and ask, "What are you doing, raising the Helium Stick instead of lowering it?!"). For added drama, jump up and pull it down!

Participants may initially be confused about the paradoxical behavior of the Helium Stick. The secret (keep it to yourself) is that the collective upwards pressure tends to be greater than the weight of the stick. Often, the more a group tries, the more it floats. Some groups or individuals (most often larger-size groups) tend to give up after 5 to 10 minutes of trying, thinking it's not possible or too hard. The facilitator can offer direct suggestions or suggest the group stops the task, discusses its strategy, and then has another go.

Less often, a group may appear to be succeeding too fast. In response, be particularly vigilant about fingers not touching the pole. Also make sure participants lower the pole all the way onto the ground. You can increase the difficulty by adding a large washer to each end of the stick, and explain that if the washers fall off during the exercise, it has to restart. Eventually the group needs to calm down, concentrate, and very slowly and patiently lower the Helium Stick—easier said than done.

Debriefing

Did everyone understand the mission and technical lowering rules?

Did anyone intentionally try to sabotage the group's mission by lifting the stick?

Did everyone sincerely want to accomplish the mission? Did you think it could be done?

If everyone understood the mission, and was committed to succeeding, why did the group get so far off track right away?

Try to elicit answers that are related to the group process, not the technical explanation of the challenge (e.g., "We didn't plan well" more so than "We weren't holding our fingers correctly").

Ask participants to share example of groups they have participated with in "the real world" that seemed to be comprised of committed folks, but were not productive.

Discuss what types of actions are important to keep a group focused on the mission.

Many times during this activity, people become frustrated with others who aren't lowering the stick, and often choose one person as the culprit. Also, some people give up and let the stick come off their fingers. If either happens, be prepared to discuss how blame or giving up affects groups.

Instant Replay

Contributor/History

This is from the New Games Foundation's book, *More New Games.*

Concept/Objective

This introductory icebreaker activity involves mirroring and overt mimicry.

Props/Materials Needed/Preparation

No props needed.

Directions/Scenarios/Instructions

- Have group members circle-up. Tell them that this activity is designed to help them get to know one another better.

- The object of this activity is for people to introduce themselves by saying their name accompanied by a gesture or body movement that represents them. Begin by giving an example, putting yourself out there first.

- Then, in unison, the rest of the group mimics the movement and the way the person said her name, exactly as she said it (or as close as possible!). Have fun with it; the more closely and purely the group mimics, the more fun this game becomes.

This activity can be carried out by having people stay where they already are (on the outside of the circle), or you can invite people to center stage for their performance (center of the circle). Either way, be consistent throughout the activity. This will ensure that the "star performers," those who are less inhibited, will not steal the spotlight of those who are a bit more reserved.

King Frog

Contributor/History

Origin Unknown. We learned this game from Star Logan at Renbrook Summer Adventure many years ago. It is also written up in the Project Adventure book, *No Props* by Mark Collard.

Concept/Objective

This is a focusing activity because you need to pay attention to learn and remember everyone's animals and motions or gestures.

Props/Materials Needed/Preparation

No props needed.

Directions/Scenarios/Instructions

- Have the group sit in a circle, and begin by having everyone think of an animal.

- Tell the group that you are King Frog and show them your hand motion (I usually slap my hands together, shooting the top hand out in front, simulating a frog jumping off a lily pad).

- Have everyone take turns naming their animals and giving a corresponding motion. It doesn't necessarily have to be a motion that one might normally associate with that animal—creativity is definitely welcomed! After each person says his or her animal and gives a corresponding motion, review the previous ones as well.

- The object of the game is to pass an impulse throughout the circle by the motions previously demonstrated. As King Frog, start the game by saying, "King Frog" and making your motion, followed by the name and motion of another player's animal. That sends the impulse to the other player. That player must receive it by repeating his/her own animal name and motion and then saying someone else's while doing the corresponding motion, and so on, and so on.

Variations

This can also be played as a competitive round. The game proceeds as described above until someone makes an error. At this point, the person who made the mistake moves to sit to the immediate right side of the King Frog. The King Frog position is now the desired seat to be in. Everyone else will shift one seat to the right. The first level of this variation simply involves moving to the desired seat (the King Frog's initial seat).

The next level would be played the same way, except the animal names and corresponding motions stay with the spots where they began. So, as people make mistakes and the group moves to new spots, they change their animal and motion to that of the person who was there before them.

Micro-Macro Wave Stretch

Contributor/History

Origin Unknown.

Concept/Objective

This is a group warm-up that provides another opportunity for some overt mimicry, for which our mirror neurons begin to do a happy getting-to-know-you dance.

Props/Materials Needed/Preparation

No props needed.

Directions/Scenarios/Instructions

- Have the participants get into a circle. Raise your hands up over your head and bring them down again, beginning that ballpark classic, "The Wave." Get everyone to play along and keep it going until everyone has bought in and the wave has gone around the group a few times.

- Now tell them you are going to have each of them, one at a time, introduce a new stretch to the group. Explain that they will alternate between two stretches. The first stretch (macro), will target a large muscle group; such as bending at the waist and touching your toes, stretching your quads, or raising your arms over your head and bending sideways, stretching your sides, etc. The next stretch (micro), will target a small muscle group; wiggling your ears, doing finger calisthenics, etc. The stretches will need to follow that pattern, macro, micro, macro, micro, until everyone has introduced at least one stretch.

- Once someone introduces the stretch, the others, much like they did for the wave, will need to wait to begin to do the stretch until the person on their right begins to do it, so we create the "wave stretch." Have everyone hold each stretch until the wave comes around and everyone has done it. Now, the next person introduces her stretch, continuing to use the alternate pattern, macro, micro, macro, micro, until the entire group has had an opportunity to lead at least one stretch and the wave has gone all the way around the group.

One Duck
Fell Into the Pond
Ker-Plunk!

Contributor/History

This is a variation on the game "One Duck" from the Project Adventure book *No Props* by Mark Collard.

Concept/Objective

Group members recite one part of the sentence, "One duck fell into the pond ker-plunk," broken down syllabically until the sentence is complete. The sentence multiplies each time it is completed until a mistake is made and the group starts over.

Props/Materials/Prep

No props needed! Minimum of 5 people, maximum of 15.

Directions/Scenarios/Instructions

*   Have group members get into a circle and ask them to repeat the sentence, "One duck fell into the pond ker-plunk." When you say the sentence, place emphasis on each syllable, as that is how the sentence will be broken down ("One–duck–fell–in–to–the–pond–ker–plunk"). Have the group repeat it after you.

*   The next step is to have group members repeat the sentence again, each saying only one word or syllable of the sentence in a clockwise direction around the circle. For instance, the first person will say, "one," the next, "duck," and so on until the sentence is complete.

- The second round begins upon completion of the sentence. The second and subsequent rounds look like this: For each new round, the words/syllables are repeated to match the round number. For example, in round two, the next person in sequence after the sentence was completed would start again with "one." The next person would repeat, "one," followed by the next person who would say "duck," who would be followed by the person on his/her left who would repeat, "duck," and so on. So, round three would have three repeats, four would have four, you get the picture.

When someone gets confused and messes up (and they will!), we tell them that we will gently remind them that they made a mistake by making the obnoxious "game show buzzer noise." At that point, the game starts over at round one, beginning with the person next in the order. The game show buzzer noise adds an element of fun, but you may want to preface it by having a quick talk about mistakes. Encourage groups to have fun, but keep in mind that everyone makes mistakes all the time. When was the last time anyone had a perfect day? I think I had one once, but I may be mistaken! Point out that it is really no big deal and that the game just keeps going on. Kind of like the rest of our lives when we make mistakes; life doesn't stop, we just pick ourselves up and keep going.

Notice the focus that can happen during this activity!

Photo Finish

Contributor/History

From *Feeding the Zircon Gorilla* by Sam Sikes. This activity may also have been called Step Over the Line.

Concept/Objective

This is a low-level group problem-solving initiative, which has a distinct focusing quality.

Props/Materials Needed/Preparation

You will need a starting point and an ending point. Using rope or a line of tape on a floor can create these, or if you are on a playing surface of some sort, use existing lines.

Directions/Scenarios/Instructions

- Tell group members that they need to line up behind the starting line. The object is to cross the space between the starting and finish lines, crossing the finish line at EXACTLY the same time as the rest of the group. Note the caps on EXACTLY!

  This sounds much easier than it is. For each attempt, the group must start back at the starting point and cross the distance between the two lines. This activity becomes a great focuser! It is so simple, yet groups really get into it.

- As the facilitator, it is your job to be the camera. Call it as you see it. If a group member is unable to participate in the traditional role for this activity, that person could play the role of camera.

Variations

- Another way to frame this one is to set it up the same exact way, but tell group members they have only one attempt at crossing the finish line. I have seen groups spend over 10 minutes planning and talking this one through, only to fail beautifully on their one attempt, having never thought to practice their decided upon methods at the starting line!

- A few higher-tech variations involve actually taking a photo, or even video of the finish. If this is the case, a Polaroid instant camera is good. A digital still or video camera works well if you have something larger than the tiny screen on the camera to view it on. We are fortunate to have a few mobile SmartBoards where we work, but a laptop screen would do just fine. If the picture is not big enough to clearly see, it is not worth doing this variation. The beautiful thing about using an actual camera is that the heat is off you!

Pipeline

Contributor/History

Pipeline is a classic team-building initiative that was originally written up as Half-Pipe in *FUNN 'n Games* by Karl Rohnke.

Concept/Objective

Pipeline is an object-transfer activity wherein the group attempts to move a round object of some sort, usually a marble or small ball, from point A to point B without dropping it.

Props/Materials Needed/Preparation

For the classic variation of Pipeline, you will need as many sections of the pipeline as you have participants. Make or purchase 12- to 18-inch long sections of PVC pipe cut down the middle to make half pipes. Now, of course you can go as crazy as you'd like with the length, but the 12- to 18-inch long sections pack really well. (A less-expensive but not as durable alternative is to use leftover paper towel or wrapping paper tubes, cut lengthwise down the middle.)

You also need a round object small enough to fit inside the pipeline. A shooter marble is our preferred object, but we have also used golf balls, ping-pong balls, toy eggs, real eggs, whatever you think would be good for the group you are working with. A bucket or container is needed to deposit the marble into at the ending of the activity. You will also need to mark a starting point (e.g., an orange floor spot).

As we mentioned in chapter 4, the end of this activity has major mirror neuron party potential. A container that has a decent tone to it, some sort of cylindrical or tube-like container, will produce the perfect "plunk" if the group is successful.

Directions/Scenarios/Instructions

- Ask the group to circle-up at the starting point and hand out the sections of pipeline. Tell the group members that their objective is to transport the marble from the starting point to the ending point using only their individual sections of pipeline.

- Once the marble is in motion in the first pipeline, it must maintain forward momentum. If it stops or rolls backwards, the activity starts over at the starting point.

- While the marble is in each person's section of pipe, that person may not move his/her feet.

- The marble cannot touch any part of any of the players at any point. This includes clothing. If the marble is touched, the activity begins again from the starting point.

- If the marble falls off of the pipeline, the activity starts over.

- There are many ways to frame this activity. We often tell participants that the marble is the symbol for their group and that they are responsible for its safe delivery to the end. We have also used this with a first-year seminar course that we teach where we framed it as getting through the first semester at college.

Debriefing

Pipeline always brings up great opportunities to discuss planning and strategies for how to best do that, as well as discussions about individual responsibility and mutual accountability.

Feel free to attach whatever metaphor will suit you and the program you are running. We have spun this one so many ways and it never gets old. Groups, both young and old, love this one. Be creative and have fun with it.

There is something to be said about allowing groups to fail if they are going to anyway. Hopefully, you would only allow this to happen if you were going to provide the group with another opportunity to test what it learned from the bumbled pipeline—"fail forward" and achieve success in subsequent initiatives. It is a real bummer to send groups off into the sunset having failed at Pipeline at the end of the day! If you choose to save this one for the end of your program, we suggest having a variation handy to allow the group its mirror neuron party plunk.

Variations

- There will be those groups who just are never going to be able to complete this activity because of time constraints, or simply because as a group, they're not going to get there. Depending on whether or not it will be beneficial for them to actually complete it, you may wish to add some opportunities for them to have their starting line up with them as they move. This can be done by setting an amount of sections the marble must travel through before the line can move up, or you can have some other "Let's Make a Deal" type of scenario that they can make use of. One of our favorite little deal-makers is a set of what we call "The Dice of Doom." These are just a set of cubed beanbags, the type that came in the original *Juggling for the Complete Klutz* book. On them we have written in silver marker things like "Animal Speak," "Rhyme Time," "Opera Speak," "Silence," as well as a few more. These are easy to make and can add a whole different dynamic to the activity, while allowing for some concessions to the original set of rules, as far as the starting point is concerned.

- Another great variation, from Chris Cavert and Sam Sikes' book, *50 Ways to Use Your Noodle*, is to use pool noodles to create the pipeline. To do this variation, each participant is given a noodle, and must pair with at least one other person to create a track for the object to roll on. Sometimes threesomes work even better together in order to contain the ball. If you are going to try this version, you will also need a ball bigger than just a marble. A baseball-sized squeeze ball or a rubber Pinky ball work well for the Noodle Pipeline. One of the really neat things about the Noodle Pipeline is that the noodles are flexible, allowing the pipelines to bend and curve. This can come in handy, especially if the group is in a confined space with some turns to make along the way, or if it just plain old overshoot its goal.

Positive Isometrics

Contributor/History

The origin of this activity is unknown. Joyce Saltman introduced this particular version, though we're not sure what she calls it, at the 2009 CAPSEF (Connecticut Association of Private Special Education Facilities) Annual Conference.

Concept/Objective

This is a very powerful visual to illustrate the impact words can have on us, both positive and negative.

Props/Materials Needed/Preparation

No props needed.

Directions/Scenarios/Instructions

- Ask for a volunteer from the group (we will assume it is a woman). Have her stand up straight with one arm extended from the shoulder, straight out to the side, with her palm open facing down. Tell her that you are going to push down on her arm and that she needs to resist and not allow you to push it down. Now, don't go too crazy here, but give it some pressure; make sure she is giving good resistance. Do this for no more than 10 to 20 seconds.

- Now, tell the group that you are going to say some negative things about the volunteer. Tell the volunteer to keep her arm up, and then make some negative statements about her, even if they are very general. Say them out loud, in a somewhat chastising way, in the ear on the same side of the body as arm that she has extended. After you say these negative things about her, tell her to resist as you push down on her arm. This time, the arm should push down fairly easily.

- Now you have a chance to redeem yourself with this person! Explain to her, and the group, that in no way, shape, or form did you believe or mean anything that you just said about her. Express some very positive, uplifting and empowering statements about now, and without taking a breath between your last positive affirmation and the next instruction, tell her to put her arm back out and resist you again. This time the volunteer is usually far more able to resist your pushing than even the first attempt, before there was anything said about her.

Debriefing

This is a wonderful activity to use to discuss the power of words and intentions. I have used this in a very elementary way with some of our special-education students. We talk about the power of positive thinking and the power that their words hold, for themselves and with others, both positive and negative. We have seen this work with kids and adults alike and while it probably has more to do with actual isometrics, when coupled with discussions about kindness and respect, positivity, and the power of belief in oneself, it can be a great conversation piece.

Variations

This activity can be done without all of the discussion, of course! One common way, and a favorite among teenage boys, is to do it the same way, but after the initial resistance, wave your hand in a circular motion in front of the person's face, then push his arm down again.

Run, Shout, Knock Yourself Out

Contributor/History

This is from Karl Rohnke's *FUNN 'n Games*.

Concept/Objective

This is a great focuser. It can be an energizer for groups who need something to wake them up or snap them out of an after-lunch food coma. It offers an opportunity to blow off some steam, creating an opportunity to mellow down in order to be able to focus. It is beautiful in its duality! It also can be helpful in teaching people how to make themselves heard if they are ever lost in the woods.

Props/Materials Needed/Preparation

No props needed, just a starting point.

Directions/Scenarios/Instructions

- In a large, open area, have the group line up in a horizontal line, facing the direction that will provide the greatest amount of distance to be covered. Stand between the group members and the expanse of space you will be using and instruct them to breathe very deeply. I usually talk a bit about proper diaphragmatic breathing and how important it is for stress reduction, as well as for optimal vocal production and projection.

- While the participants are practicing, tell them that in a minute, after you finish giving the instructions, they will take three deep breaths. After the third deep breath, they will, in one breath, run as far as they can, screaming as loud as they can, stopping wherever their breath runs out. Make sure that you point out that this is only a competition against themselves, since we all have varying lung capacities and we don't intend this to be a contest.

Variations

As mentioned above, this can be good to energize a group, to snap out of that food coma, or first thing in the morning to get the system going.

It can also be a great activity to help kids wind down a bit! I remember using this one summer with a group of sixth-grade boys who were practically bouncing off the walls when they came up to the ropes course. This was fine when we were playing games, but when it got to group work and problem solving, they couldn't focus. So, I had them do this and they loved it so much, they wanted to run the entire length of a soccer field and back, twice! I figured, "Why not?" When they returned to the log circle, having blown off lots of steam, they were ready to focus, listen, and solve some problems together!

Snoopy vs. The Red Baron

Contributor/History

This is another classic from Karl Rohnke's *Silver Bullets*.

Concept/Objective

This is a warm-up activity that can get our bodies moving and our mirror neurons firing like WWI fighter pilots.

Props/Materials Needed/Preparation

No props needed.

Directions/Scenarios/Instructions

- Have everyone find a partner. Ask them to pick between them who will be Snoopy and who will be the Red Baron.

- Have everyone face his or her partner, standing about an arm's length away from each other, so they can reach out and just barely tap the partner's shoulder. Tell them to stand with their feet spread shoulder-width apart and to keep their feet in one place.

- Ask the partners to decide which hand they will play with and to open that hand flat, folding the thumb in, as though they were going to salute, but pointing their fingers out toward their partner. This hand has become the fighter plane. The object is for whomever decided to be the Red Baron to try to tag

Snoopy, while Snoopy tries to elude the Red Baron—all of this being done without moving your feet. Once a tag has been made, the roles switch, and now it is Snoopy doing the chasing. Encourage the group to really go for it and make fighter plane sounds, both engines and artillery.

Variations

Another way to do this activity is to allow group members to move their feet. If you use this variation, have them extend their arms out to their sides like wings and chase like that, making sure they are continuing to make airplane sounds and switching roles when a tag is made.

Webbing Yurt Circle

Contributor/History

This is a variation of the activity Yurt Rope that is in *Quicksilver* by Karl Rohnke and Steve Butler.

Concept/Objective

The object is for the group to lean and shift its weight, using a piece of 1-inch webbing and pulling force in such a way as to maintain equilibrium while all sitting and then rising as a team.

Props/Materials Needed/Preparation

You will need a length of 1-inch diameter webbing, allowing about 2 feet of webbing per participant. Secure the ends with a water knot. This can also be done with synthetic rope of at least 5/8-inch diameter, but the webbing seems to be easier on people's hands. This can be done in any indoor or outdoor space that is free from obstructions and has solid footing.

Directions/Scenarios/Instructions

- Ask all the members to stand outside the circle of webbing and pick it up with both hands. Their feet should be a shoulder's-width apart.

- On an agreed signal, everyone should start to lean backwards against the strength of the webbing. They should slowly bend their knees until everyone makes posterior contact with the grass/floor at about the same time.

- After congratulating each other on such a coordinated series of two-point landings, ask the group to try to stand together, while keeping the tension on the rope.

Debriefs

Possible debriefs include talking about individual and group focus, outside forces pulling you down or in, and the sense of team spirit that comes from a shared physical common activity.

Write Together

Contributor/History

We originally saw a variation of Bull Ring (p. 73) during an Adventure Practitioners Symposium at High 5 Adventure Learning Center in Brattleboro, Vermont. It was in a workshop delivered by Soni Haflett, Betsi Seeley, and Mary Abreu, who are adventure facilitators from the organization called ALPS, Adventure Learning and Programming for Success.

Concept/ Objective

The objective of the activity is to have group members use the Bull Ring/Write Together platform to write or create a drawing on a piece of paper that represents them or answers a question they are given.

Props/Materials Needed/Preparation

The original concept we saw was to take an octagonal piece of half-inch plywood, about 16 inches in diameter, and attach an eye-hook to each side. Off of each eye hook is where you would string the hand lines for each group member to use to manipulate this "group writing machine." In the middle of the plywood there was a hole drilled big enough for a magic marker to be stuck through and secured with some masking tape. After uncapping the marker, the writing machine was ready for use. Supply paper to write on.

One dimension of this prop that we noticed was that the size of the board limited the vision of the group. This can be useful at times, but also a hindrance. We came up with an alternative, using the original bull ring, that eliminates the vision problem. We decided that it was more conducive to group focus to have all the participants be able to see the product they were producing.

The variation we use involves modifying an old 2.5-inch diameter squeeze ball. Using an awl, and then a Phillips-head screwdriver, I poked a hole through the center of the squeeze ball. Make the hole big enough so that you can work a Sharpie through it. There still needs to be enough tension from the ball to secure the pen though. Once the pen is resting midway through the ball, just squeeze the ball into the middle of a bull ring that has been made with a 2.5-inch diameter ring. This can then be used to create the image on the piece of paper you supply for the group.

Directions/Scenarios/Instructions

- Ask the group members to pick up their end of the string. Explain that the object is to apply some tension to the strings, and write on the paper.

- At this point, to help the participants focus, have them draw an image that is fairly simple, perhaps a square or a triangle. Let them practice with the cap on, before removing it for the final try. Since all participants can see, it becomes easier for the group members to focus and work together as they create.

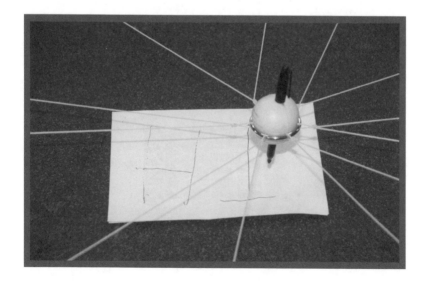

Debriefs

A possible debrief would be to ask the group members if they noticed a difference in their reactions between when they had to give more tension and when they had to remove some tension as the shape of drawing was being created. In the original Bull Ring progression, group members are indeed pulling in opposite directions to provide the required tension, but they are all moving in similar directions to solve the challenge. When participating in Write Together, members must, at times, move in opposite directions in concert with other participants, in order to solve the problem. That give and take could spark discussions for a rich reflection from the participants about the way they work together under normal circumstances.

Yurt Circle

Contributor/History

This activity comes from the original *Cowstails and Cobras* by Karl Rohnke. A yurt is a temporary but quite strong building of nomadic tribes in the Middle East and Asia. When properly constructed, it can withstand a great deal of outside force from nature. They are round and well balanced.

Concept/Objective

The objective is to have group members join hands and form a circle that supports itself when alternate members lean their bodies inward and outward.

Props/Materials Needed/Preparation

No props are needed for this activity, but it does require an even number of participants. Safety precautions include using a flat space with good traction and having participants remove any rings that might put undue pressure on their neighbors' hands.

Directions/Scenarios/Instructions

- Have group members stand in a circle, facing inward. Ask them to join hands, palm to palm, without interlocking any fingers. Decide on a method of signaling when the group should begin.

- Explain that the object is for alternate people to lean either inwards or outwards, while supporting the participants on each side of them. It is beneficial to discuss group strategies and body posture to use during this activity. It is important to keep your body locked in a straight line. This way, the pressure that each of your neighbors feel as you lean remains relatively steady. This makes it easier for your neighbors to adjust to any weight differential they may feel. The key to keeping your body straight is twofold. First, lean slowly. Second, keep your legs stiff and use your core muscles to rotate your pelvis into a forward position.

• See if the group members can stabilize themselves for 5 seconds with their feet stationary. Then, have the group switch who leans in and who leans out. Warn the group that this is not an Olympic event. Should you totally lose your balance, let go with your hands so that you can catch yourself.

Debriefs

This activity lends itself well to the discussion that you always need support, from both sides, or from in front of you as well as from behind you, as you move through the pictures that are your days or through the film that is your life.

Focus Your Locus Conclusion

There are many models of the experiential learning cycle, all of which contain stages that represent an idea, an experience, the processing of that experience, and the transfer of that new knowledge. The application of the focus cycle complements and enhances one's progress along the experiential learning cycle, either opening or narrowing one's lens, according to the stage one is in. It has been our experience that the mixing of this theory with activities that produce the positive effects of play is what will help groups to perform more effectively and individuals to focus their locus.

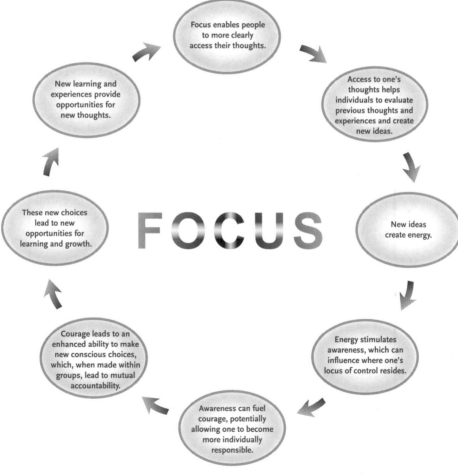

Focus enables people to more clearly access their thoughts.

Access to one's thoughts helps individuals to evaluate previous thoughts and experiences and create new ideas.

New ideas create energy.

Energy stimulates awareness, which can influence where one's locus of control resides.

Awareness can fuel courage, potentially allowing one to become more individually responsible.

Courage leads to an enhanced ability to make new conscious choices, which, when made within groups, lead to mutual accountability.

These new choices lead to new opportunities for learning and growth.

New learning and experiences provide opportunities for new thoughts.

FOCUS

About the Authors

In the late 1970s, MIKE GESSFORD was fortunate to have a quality challenge ropes course experience at Nauset Regional High School during PE class. Using that as a springboard, and pursuing further coursework in adventure education, he graduated from Plymouth State University with a Bachelor's degree in Physical Education. He earned a Master's degree in PE from Central Connecticut State University.

Mike has enjoyed being the physical education teacher at the Gengras Center since 1987. The Gengras Center is a top-rated, private, special-education facility, serving approximately 125 students ages 5 to 21 on the campus of Saint Joseph College in West Hartford, Connecticut. Ten years ago Mike began using adventure-education methods in PE classes to provide hands-on learning experiences for the older students. In the role of Adventure Education Coordinator for Saint Joseph College, Mike has worked with Justin to expand this pedagogy into the college community, using experiential activities and their challenge ropes course. Mike facilitates many diverse types of user groups at the challenge course and works as part of a great team on the challenge course at Renbrook Summer Adventure.

Mike's passion for adventure/experiential learning and teaching has helped him to successfully share these methods with students, teachers, and administrators of all learning styles and experience. He enjoys the opportunity to present these techniques and activities at numerous local, state, regional, and international conferences. Mike is grateful for opportunities to share what he has learned from his students and teachers alike.

Mike learned early that, by staying open to what is possible, he seemed to have moments of personal clarity that became very important to who he is today. As Mike continues exploring this magical life, he hopes that, by staying in the present, the moments of serendipity continue to reveal themselves to him. And, by sharing those with people around him, their lives can take on new meaning as well.

Mike lives happily in Simsbury, Connecticut.

mgessford@sjc.edu
(860) 231-5479 office

 JUSTIN MCGLAMERY is a visionary and cre-
ative thinker whose quest for lifelong learning
fuels the many divergent passions he brings
to his work and to his life. Justin teaches at
Saint Joseph College using experiential/ad-
venture education as a pedagogical approach
with many different populations and for many
different reasons. For the past 15 years, he
has worked with students with special needs
at he Gengras Center School of Saint Joseph
College. Since 2001, Justin has been facilitating therapeutic adventure-education sessions
for students and providing team-building workshops and in-services for
staff. For the past five years, Justin has cotaught several courses at the
college including a first-year seminar course called T.E.A.M., a Group
Dynamics course, and adventure education for physical education credit.
In addition to undergraduate curriculum courses, Justin facilitates team-
building programs for many of the various departments and groups on
campus, as well as for corporate groups, school groups, and athletic
teams from the larger outside community.

Justin has presented at many regional, national, and international conferences, promoting the use of experiential activities to engage learners and
enhance teaching. Justin received the 2009 Educator of the Year award
from the Connecticut Association for Private Special Education Facilities,
an honor he is proud to share with his coauthor and partner in adventure,
Mike Gessford.

In addition to his passion for teaching and learning with people, Justin is
a musician, poet, actor, and activist. His love of life and laughter fuels his
daily life and Justin seeks and creates fun wherever he goes.

Justin lives in an old fixer-upper home in a historic neighborhood in
Hartford, Connecticut with his loving wife and best friend, Jarrad, and his
three wonderful and inspiring children.

jmcglamery@sjc.edu
(860) 231-5790 office

References

Altschuler, E., Pineda, J., & Ramachandran, V. S. (2000). *Mirror neurons: How we become what we see.* Abstracts of the Annual Meeting of the Society for Neuroscience.

(2001). *American heritage dictionary.* Boston, MA: Houghton Mifflin Co.

Anderson, M., Cain, J., Heck, T., & Cavert, C. (2005). *Teambuilding puzzles: 100 puzzles and activities for creating teachable moments.* Fundoing Publications.

Belenky, M., Clinchy, B., Goldberger, N. & Tarule, J. (1997). *Women's ways of knowing: The development of self, voice, and mind.* New York: Basic Books.

Broussard, Chris (2007, November 1). A fresh coat. *ESPN The Magazine.* Retrieved October 24, 2008, from http://sports.espn. go.com/nba/news/story?page=mag-celtics.

Cain, J. & Jolliff, B. (1997). *Teamwork & teamplay: A guide to cooperative, challenge, and adventure activities.* Dubuque, IA: Kendall/Hunt Publishing Co.

Cain, J., Cummings, M., & Stanchfield, J. (2008). *A teachable moment: A facilitator's guide to activities for processing, debriefing, reviewing and reflection.* Dubuque, IA: Kendall/Hunt Publishing Co.

Carey, B. (2008, February 12). You remind me of me. *The New York Times.* Retrieved October 24, 2008, from http://nytimes. com/2008/02/12/health/12mimic.html.

Cavert, C. & Sikes, S. (1997). *50 ways to use your noodle: Loads of land games with foam noodle toys.* Tulsa, OK: Learning Unlimited Corp.

Collard, M. (2005). *No props: Great games with no equipment.* Beverly, MA: Project Adventure, Inc.

Emoto, M. (2008). *The healing power of water.* Hay House, Inc.

Gallwey, W. T. (1977). *The inner game of tennis.* New York: Random House Publishing.

Gardner, H. (1993). *Frames of mind: The theory of multiple intelligences.* New York: Basic Books.

Goldberg, C., & Globe Staff (2005, December 12). We feel your pain... and your happiness too: The human brain's source of empathy may also play a role in autism. *The Boston Globe*.

Iacoboni, M. (2008). *Mirroring people: The new science of how we connect with others*. New York: Farrar, Straus and Giroux.

Iacoboni, M., Molnar-Szakacs, I., Gallese, V., Buccino, G., Mazziotta, J. C. et al. (2005). Grasping the intentions of others with one's own mirror neuron system. *PLoS Biol, 3*(3): e79.

Jacobson, M. & Ruddy, M. (2004). *Open to outcome: A practical guide for facilitating and teaching experiential reflection*. Bethany, OK: Wood 'N' Barnes.

Keyes, K., Jr. (1982). *The hundredth monkey*. Coos Bay, OR: Vision Books.

Lencioni, P. (July, 2008). *Pat's point of view*. The Table Group. Retrieved July 30, 2008, from http://www.thetablegroup.com/pat/povs/

New Games Foundation. (1976). *The new games book: Play hard, play fair, nobody hurt*. San Francisco, CA: Main Street Books.

New Games Foundation. (1981). *More new games*. San Francisco, CA: Main Street Books.

Peck, M. S. (1998). *The different drum: Community making and peace*. New York: Touchstone.

Ramachandran, V. S. (2000, May 29). Mirror neurons and imitation learning as the driving force behind "the great leap forward" in human evolution. *Edge*, 69.

Robinson, B. A. (2008). *Shared belief in the "Golden Rule."* Retrieved April 12, 2009, from http://www.religioustolerance.org/reciproc.htm.

Robinson, G. & Rose, M. (2007). *Teams for a new generation: A facilitator's field guide*. Bloomington, IN: AuthorHouse.

Rohnke, K. (1977). *Cowstails and cobras: A guide to ropes courses, initiative games, and other adventure activities*. Hamilton, MA: Project Adventure.

Rohnke, K. (1980). *Cowstails and cobras II: A guide to games, initiatives, ropes courses, & adventure curriculum*. Dubuque, IA: Kendall/Hunt Publishing Co.

Rohnke, K. (1984). *Silver bullets: A guide to initiative problems, adventure games, and trust activities*. Dubuque, Iowa: Project Adventure, Kendall Hunt Publishing Co.

Rohnke, K. (1994). *The Bottomless Bag Again*. Dubuque, Iowa:Kendall/ Hunt Publishing Co.

Rohnke, K. (1996). *FUNN stuff, Vol. 1*. Dubuque, IA: Kendall/Hunt Publishing Co.

Rohnke, K. (2004). *FUNN 'n games*. Dubuque, IA: Kendall/Hunt Publishing Co.

Rohnke, K. & Bulter, S. (1995). *Quicksilver: Adventure games, initiative problems, trust activities and a guide to effective leadership*. Dubuque, IA: Kendall/Hunt Publishing Co.

Schoel, J., Prouty, D., & Radcliffe, P. (1995). *Islands of healing: A guide to adventure based counseling*. Dubuque, IA: Kendall/Hunt Publishing Co.

Seaward, B. L. (2008). *Managing stress: Principles and strategies for health and well-being*. Jones & Bartlett Publishers.

Shoemaker, F. (1997). *Extraordinary golf: The art of the possible*. New York: Perigee Books.

Sikes, S. (1995). *Feeding the zircon gorilla and other team building activities*. Tulsa, OK: Learning Unlimited Corp.

Sikes, S. (2003). *Raptor and other team building activities*. Tulsa, OK: Learning Unlimited Corp.

Simpson, S. (2003). *The leader who is hardly known: Self-less teaching from the Chinese tradition*. Bethany, OK: Wood 'N' Barnes.

Simpson, S., Miller, D., & Bocher, B. (2006). *The processing pinnacle: An educator's guide to better processing*. Bethany, OK: Wood 'N' Barnes Publishing.

Stanchfield, J. (2008). *Tips & Tools: The art of experiential group facilitation*. Bethany, OK: Wood 'N' Barnes Publishing.

Tuckman, B. (1965). Developmental sequence of small groups. *Psychological Bulletin, 63*: 384-399.

Warren, K. (1996). *Women's voices in experiential education*. Dubuque, IA: Kendall/Hunt Publishing Co.

Weinstein, M. & Goodman, J. (1980). *Playfair: Everybody's guide to noncompetitive play*. San Luis Obisbo, CA: Impact Publishers.

Index